MW00884102

ALL IN:

How To Become An Overnight Rock 'n' Roll Roadie Success In Just 20 Years

JEFF MANN

Printed by CreateSpace.com
In the United States of America
Published in 2017 by The Real Jeff Mann Publishing
Inquiries: jeffreyjohnmann@gmail.com
http://therealjeffmann.com

ISBN: 1974266885
ISBN-13: 978-1974266883

DEDICATION

If there’s one thing rock 'n' roll roadies are good at, its telling stories. Let's face it, lots of crazy stuff happens when you send a bunch of overgrown man-children around the world with a rock band and supply them with copious amounts of free time and disposable income. Every time I told one of my hilariously insightful roadie stories, someone invariably said, "You know, you should write a book!"

After hearing this for years I finally got inspired to actually DO IT. There were a few different motivating factors that led to my decision to become an author. First and foremost, an old roadie brother of mine, Ken Barr, went ahead and did it first. Ken's book, "We Are The Road Crew", is a fun read that details his adventures touring the world with a whole bunch of big time rock bands. Seeing him do it really inspired me.

Secondly, writing a book is something most people never do. At this point in my life, my goal is to live as fully as possible in the time I have left on this planet, and the idea of never even being brave enough to try to get the book written became unthinkable to me. I decided to at least give it a shot. I felt like my story was worth telling.

Once I actually got started, writing the book was fun. I committed to sit down to write for at least 30 minutes every day. Most days it turned out to be much longer than just 30 minutes. Once I got rolling it was hard to stop.

Thanks to the internet I was able to go back and research the parts that I had forgotten about. Or the parts I was too drunk to remember clearly. I relived a lot of fun memories during the writing process. I went over some bad memories too. Those parts weren't so much fun. I did a lot of things I am not proud of during my years on the road, and going back over those parts was challenging for me. I think it was worth reopening some of those old scars to get the story told.

This book is dedicated to everyone who goes "ALL IN" to make their dream come true. Whether your dream is to be a championship athlete, a published author, a professional porn star or a rock 'n' roll roadie, if you work hard and give it everything you've got your dream can come true. I know this is true, because it happened to me.

I hope you enjoy reading about my journey from a young kid in the wilderness of upstate New York dreaming about being a rock star to an older, (hopefully) wiser grownup looking back on the crazy adventures I had as I traveled all over the world living my dream.

-Jeff Mann

Tucson, Arizona

November 2017

CONTENTS

1	IN THE BEGINNING	1
2	LOST HORIZON	7
3	MASTERS OF REALITY	16
4	THINGS GET SUICIDAL	27
5	THE PLAGUE THAT MAKES YOUR BOOTY MOVE	35
6	WELCOME TO EUROPE. NOW, GO HOME	41
7	EUROPEAN ROCK FESTIVALS ARE A GREAT WAY TO MAKE FRIENDS	48
8	I COME FROM A LAND DOWN UNDER	55
9	TOURING WITH METALLICA (AGAIN, SOME MORE)	63
10	RACISM, SEXISM, AND OTHER -ISMS	73
11	WE'RE NOT WORTHY	76
12	ALICE COOPER IS ACTUALLY A REALLY, REALLY NICE GUY	92
13	THE AMERICAN DREAM IS ALIVE AND WELL	99
14	CLOWN SUITS AND SNAKE POOP	101
15	MEET THE NEW BOSS, SAME AS THE OLD BOSS (EXCEPT WITH DIFFERENT DRUM STICKS)	106
16	DEAD BABIES, DEAD BODIES AND HOW TO GET YOURSELF KILLED ON TOUR	109

17	HELLO, NEW MILLENNIUM	115
18	ROADIE-ING IS MY BUSINESS (AND BUSINESS IS GOOD)	119
19	WISCONSIN DEATH TRIP	132
20	TONIGHT AND THE REST OF MY LIFE (OR AT LEAST THE REST OF THIS TOUR)	137
21	YOU WANTED THE BEST (BUT THIS DRUM ROADIE IS ALL WE HAD)	141
22	IDLE HANDS ARE THE DEVILS PLAYGROUND	166
23	BACK TO MEGADETH	173
24	THIS IS THE END	190
25	EPILOGUE	198

1 IN THE BEGINNING

Doesn't every kid want to be a rock star someday? Growing up in the 1970's, the music world was fertile ground for the rock star I so desperately longed to become. Music was my thing. Listening to Led Zeppelin and Queen on the radio was the whole point of any trip in my mother's car. And there were the hip-swaying, lip-curling Elvis Presley 8-tracks at my dad's house. By the time I hit high school in the 80's, MTV was a constant obsession, because nothing was cooler than seeing rock videos full of blonde supermodels in living color on our very own TV screen. Spandex pants? Oh yeah. When I wasn't glued to the boob tube watching music videos I was listening to 95X, Syracuse's best rock 'n' roll radio station, feeding my music addiction. Finally, there was the one thing sure to set any young person firmly on the path of a life consumed by rock 'n' roll: my first AC/DC album, "Dirty Deeds Done Dirt Cheap". My mind was completely blown by the evil powers of rock 'n' roll, and it was time to get serious.

The first step on the long and winding road to rock stardom is picking an instrument. But which one? There are a lot of complicated-looking strings on a guitar or bass. Keyboards looked too much like math. I wasn't into taking lessons or practicing, but I liked hitting things, so the drums were my first choice. If Tommy Lee could hook up with Pamela Anderson playing 'em, that was definitely good enough for me. Being in a rock band was the only thing to do that didn't completely suck in the small upstate New York town I was born in. Most of the kids my age were into hunting and fishing, and that definitely wasn't where I was coming from. Showing off playing rock 'n' roll and chasing girls in mini-skirts seemed like a better way to navigate the treacherous waters of high school. Luckily my younger brother Brian took up the electric guitar and together we started the slow climb from "Total incompetence" to "Hey, those guys kinda rock."

To say I was obsessed with rock 'n' roll as a teenager would be putting it lightly. All I wanted to do all day long (and all night long, too) was listen to my favorite bands or read about my favorite bands. I was a straight "A" student in the school of rock. Needless to say, studying my favorite album covers and lyric sheets was way more important than studying for final exams. To this day I can recall the names of the members of an obscene number of obscure 80's metal bands. This knowledge is so ingrained it probably even got into my DNA somehow, which might be bad news for my son. Developing an encyclopedic knowledge of rock was a badge of honor among the music nuts I hung out with, and I amassed an impressive collection of vinyl albums during this time that I still wish I could track down today. Countless hours were spent searching through the LP bins at my favorite local music shop looking for the latest heavy metal albums. I spent so much time at that record store I ended up losing my virginity to this cute clerk who worked there.

Next up was finding the other members of the heavy metal band that was going to make all my rock 'n' roll dreams come true. This wasn't as easy as you might think. Remember, this was in the early 80's, and there was no Internet, no Facebook, no way to seek out like-minded music maniacs. Plus, I lived in the dreary wasteland of Syracuse, New York. I spent most days trudging the hallways of my high school hoping to stumble upon the next David Lee Roth waiting in the cafeteria line for Sloppy Joes. Finally, the universe spoke.

The long-haired kid with the locker next to mine came to school wearing a Saxon tee shirt one day. Saxon is a British heavy-metal band, widely accepted as one of the progenitors of the heavy metal genre and a full-fledged member of the legendary NWOBHM (New Wave Of British Heavy Metal), an elite group of seminal and wildly influential metal bands that pretty much single handedly saved rock music and inspired the rise of hard rock and heavy metal in America in the 80's. Which, depending on your point of view, is either a good thing or completely unforgivable. In any case, NWOBHM bands like Saxon, Motorhead, and Venom directly influenced US bands like Slayer, Anthrax and even the almighty Metallica, who went so far as to release an entire album's worth of cover versions of their favorite NWOBHM songs. And yes, it's true, Saxon's biggest hit song ever was a little ditty called "Denim & Leather," an ode to the default wardrobe choice of rockers everywhere! That shirt was like a traffic light changing from red to green, and I knew it was finally time to make those dreams of rock 'n' roll and trying to hook up with Pamela Anderson come true! It was such a relief to discover I wasn't the only one who was into British heavy metal bands who sang about denim and leather.

We started talking, mostly about our favorite rock bands and girls. The guy in the Saxon shirt's name was also Jeff, and providentially he and his bass-playing brother Mike were trying to start a heavy metal band. They needed a drummer and a guitarist. I had both, thanks to my little brother, who by now was shredding away on his axe like a boy-child possessed. Beer fueled living room rehearsals began immediately, and some of the worst renditions of "Iron Man" by Black Sabbath ever heard started disturbing the peace on the street where I lived. Bands like Led Zeppelin, Rush and Aerosmith were the blueprint for our early efforts at rock stardom, and eventually we started to get good. Along with developing our musical skills we started experimenting with the other excesses that seemed to naturally come with being young, dumb and full of Metallica records, like engaging in flagrant truancy and over imbibing, that all seemed to be part of the rock star package.

Much of our reckless behavior stemmed from the sheer boredom of being a teenager in Syracuse, combined with the bad influence of our role models in bands like Motley Crue and Guns & Roses. There was almost literally nothing else to do in a failing industrial town disguised as a college town besides get high and chase girls. My friends and I didn't fit in the with the jocks running around on the lacrosse field, the hillbillies shooting guns and driving pickup trucks out at the lake or the rich college crowd spending mommy and daddy's money on the Syracuse University campus. So we found our own way to get our kicks. Like the Ramones sang, "Nothing to do, nowhere to go, I wanna be sedated." I mean, doesn't everybody in high school sneak out of school to go drinking at lunch-time? These were the happiest days of my formative rock 'n' roll years as I reached some critical heavy metal milestones during this time. My brother and I played our first show together, with our speed metal band MannSlaughter. See what we did there? With the double "N"? Who says metalheads are stupid? Our first gig was with Syracuse punk rock legends The Catatonics at their farewell concert. I got my first double bass drum set, which was kind of ironic since I was having a hard enough time playing one bass drum, let alone two. But all my heavy metal drum heroes had two bass drums, so I saved up my allowance and got one too. I learned the fine art of sneaking out at night to go boozing with my buddies without getting caught. Somehow we rookie rock stars graduated from high school in spite of it all. Finally, I was free to focus on music full time.

I was dedicated to rock. I got a job at a record store which gave me access to the food of my soul. It was a pretty easy gig. I worked back in the shipping warehouse, and my main job was filling orders and shipping product. Back in those days, drugstores like Walgreens and CVS stocked a small assortment of CDs and cassette tapes. It was mostly pop hits (think Culture Club and Madonna) but with some classic rock mixed in too. And don't forget those golden oldies like Captain & Tennille and my old favorite Elvis Presley, he of the inspirational pelvic thrusts. It was a horribly boring gig, perfect for someone who was perpetually hungover. A favorite pastime for us shipping clerks was trying to sneak something cool in with all the cheesy stuff on the orders we were packing. Hopefully I was able to change someone's life for the better by putting those Soundgarden albums in with their orders.

Besides trying to educate the world about Seattle rock 'n' roll bands, I played in bands. I went to shows. And, fatefully, I began working as a "roadie" for my friends' bands at their gigs.

2 LOST HORIZON

Helping my buddies at their club gigs granted me an all access pass to a whole new level of rock 'n' roll. The biggest rock club in town was the Lost Horizon, and whenever I got a chance I'd be there carrying amps and helping set up the stage for the local bands I hung around with. My dedication to rock 'n' roll and my ability to carry heavy things caught the eye of Scott Sterling. Scott was the sound guy at the Lost Horizon, and played guitar in one of the coolest bands in Syracuse, Rockin' Bones. He offered me a few jobs helping load in equipment for the big national bands that came through town to play at the Lost. The idea of getting paid to hang around backstage at a big rock show and carry drums seemed like a dream come true to a young rocker like myself, so I eagerly accepted his offer.

The Lost Horizon was a rundown rock club on the East side of Syracuse that had definitely seen better days. The dressing room was covered in spray painted graffiti, the DJ booth was awash in empty beer bottles and cigarette butts, and the restrooms...well, let's just say you only used them if you had absolutely no other choice. The place was smoky, drafty, dirty and dingy, but to me it was the coolest place in the world. At the Lost Horizon I got to hang around with rockers, drink beer, chase girls, and live out my dreams of rock stardom. It was basically Disneyland for a young rocker with overactive hormones and an addiction to rock 'n' roll.

I quickly learned the intricacies of being a stagehand. That's the fancy name they give to the people who do all the hard work at a concert - unloading trucks, moving heavy equipment, stacking speaker cabinets, and then taking it all down and putting it back into the trucks. I learned about all the different logistical configurations a rock 'n' roll tour might come in. Touring bands will usually have a tour bus and at least one truck carrying the equipment. More budget conscious groups will have to downgrade to an equipment trailer that is towed behind the tour bus. It all depends on what kind of budget they have to work with. As you move further down the food chain you will see bands that have a tour bus with the equipment carried underneath in the luggage bays, and further on down to the infamous van tour, where the band and gear all go inside one small vehicle. Some of the best shows I've ever seen were by bands on van tours. Something about living hand to mouth in a cramped, smelly van full of amps makes for awesome rock 'n' roll.

Remember, back in the late 1980's there were some amazing bands out there playing the club circuit. These weren't just local bands, but internationally touring groups with major label records. I was deeply into the burgeoning speed and thrash metal scene and getting the chance to see and hang out with some of my favorite groups was thrilling. Among the most memorable metal gigs I got to work were Anthrax, Overkill, Nuclear Assault, Kreator, Hallow's Eve, and the almighty Slayer! This job was like a dream come true for me. I tried not to bug the guys in the bands, and I never asked for autographs or anything like that. Getting to see the show from up close and maybe drink a beer with a few of my heavy metal heroes was enough for me.

ALL ACCESS
Double check all your stuff.
I was borderline obsessive compulsive about making sure my gear was right before show time. I was a double- and triple-checker. The last thing you want is something coming loose during a gig. It's embarrassing and can also lead to unemployment. Chasing a loose wing nut around on stage while pyro is going off is NOT COOL.

Scott must have liked what he saw me doing as a stagehand because he started giving me more work at the club. Learning how to set up the stage came next. Setting up the microphones and mic stands, running cables, and wiring the power amps and mixers were all part of this phase of my roadie education. Eventually I was accepted to roadie graduate school: operating the sound board and doing lights. This was the best part of the whole roadie gig because there was room for self-expression. You actually had some input! As the soundman you could decide if the guitars needed to be louder or if the vocals were too up front. When I was doing lights it was up to me if the stage should be bright or dimly shrouded in smoke. The relationship between the musicians and the roadies is an important one, and this was where I learned that a good roadie crew can make or break a band. At the Lost Horizon our crew prided itself on making even the most mediocre local garage band look and sound like a million bucks.

The only thing about the Lost Horizon that bands hated was the pole in the middle of the stage. You heard me right, smack dab in the middle of the stage was a pole from floor to ceiling. Apparently it was some sort of load bearing element and couldn't be removed or the roof would fall in. Most bands bitched relentlessly about it during their shows. I couldn't figure out why they were so bummed out about it. To me they sounded like whiny babies. Other incorporated it into their stage shows, like when Henry Rollins ceaselessly climbed around on it like monkey bars during the Black Flag shows.

Working at rock shows was turning out be just as fun as playing at rock shows. Actually it was more fun, when you factored in the fact that we usually got paid for roadie-ing. Payment for actually doing the rocking itself was much more inconsistent. Playing in rock 'n' roll bands isn't a wise financial maneuver since you're always dependent on drawing lots of people to your gigs and finding an honest club owner willing to pay you what you deserve. Roadies got just as much beer and access to girls as the guys in the bands did. My rock compass began to point more strongly towards the noble art of being a roadie. Was this a life changing moment? You bet your ass it was. I didn't know it at the time, but this was where the rock 'n' roll adventure that would literally take me around the world several times really got started.

The Lost Horizon opened in 1976 and was where I grew from a fledgling rock 'n' roller to a full grown heavy metal maniac ready to leave the nest and take on the world. It's one of the longest running club concert venues in New York state. In 40 plus years just about every band you could think of played there, and from 1988 until 1992 yours truly probably carried their amps. Among the bands that performed at the Lost are Neil Young, Guns & Roses, Raging Slab, Queen, Kiss, the Ramones, Foo Fighters, Concrete Blonde, Black Sabbath, Blue Oyster Cult, Fugazi, Slayer, Anthrax, Soundgarden, The Black Crowes, Dio, Nuclear Assault, Twisted Sister... The Lost Horizon was our rock 'n' roll clubhouse, and the coolest place in town to hang out. I could be found there abusing my employee bar tab discount seven nights a week.

Other than the Lost, the other rock 'n' roll HQ in Syracuse was a dilapidated warehouse on the North Side of town. Owned by Sam Albino, this run down old warehouse was where most of the bands in town rehearsed. Sam had divided the massive space up into dozens of rehearsal rooms which he rented out to the local rock 'n' roll bands. There must have been at least twenty bands practicing there. The sound company I worked for even stored their gear in one of the bigger rooms. If you were looking to join a band or needed to find a musician, Albino's was the place to look. Every night the place was packed with rockers writing songs, rehearsing for their next big gig, or just getting high with their buddies. Any way you slice it, it was the place to be.

Albino's burned to the ground one night in 1990. The cause of the fire was never determined, despite rumors of arson. The night of the fire I got a phone call from a friend telling me to get over there and get my stuff out. I rushed over but got there too late. My drum set and all my musical equipment was already destroyed. The whole building was engulfed in flames as fire trucks arrived to fight the fire, to no avail. Word spread and soon there must have been a hundred long haired rock 'n' rollers standing around outside watching sadly as the place went up in smoke.

Eventually my parent's house could no longer contain my rock 'n' roll lifestyle, which led to me moving out, and upstairs from Scott Sterling. His place on Westcott Street in Syracuse was rock 'n' roll central, with a constantly rotating cast of musicians and assorted entertainers coming and going at all hours of the day and night. One room-mate ran a strip-o-gram service. I was perfectly okay with that arrangement. Like an immersion program for foreign exchange students, there was simply no faster or more direct way for a young rocker to learn about the music business. Plus, living in a house full of rock 'n' rollers, roadies and strippers? I was in heaven. We had a wonderful crew of misfits working at the Lost Horizon, and they became my surrogate family as music became my whole life. For me living this way wasn't work, I was doing it because I loved it so much. Working at the record store, playing drums, listening to music, working at the Lost Horizon, watching bands play, hanging around with musicians...that was my world! 24 hours a day, 7 days a week. Talk about living your dream! Was I all in? You bet your ass I was!

Besides cutting my teeth as a tech and learning the tricks of the roadie trade I was still playing drums whenever I could, and was currently playing for a heavier than thou band called Buttzilla. Yes, it IS the greatest name for a rock ‘n’ roll band ever, isn’t it? Influenced by equal parts grunge, hardcore punk and speed metal, Buttzilla played a ton of house parties, art openings and even a few big metal fests at the famous Lost Horizon. We even managed a show at Fuoco’s Lounge, a rough joint on the North side of town where we managed to hold our own on a bill packed with speed metal bands. Buttzilla was so tough that even when one of our guitar players moved off to Arizona (Chris Johnsen, who went on to true rock ‘n’ roll glory playing with amazing bands like Camarosmith and Zeke) we just kept the party going as a power trio.

Moving to a little one room bungalow apartment down the street from the Lost Horizon was my next logical(?) move, because I was at the Lost pretty much every night as it was. Having a place within staggering distance of the club made bringing dates home a lot easier and curtailed any drunk driving incidents, to a large degree.

I was 23 when I got a gig playing drums for Uncle Sam, a hard rock band from Rochester NY, about 90 miles away from Syracuse. I answered their ad in a local music and entertainment newspaper. Our shared love of rock ‘n’ roll and drinking way too much was readily apparent. Uncle Sam had a 70's Detroit rock 'n' roll sound, kind of like a mix of Iggy & the Stooges and "Love It To Death" era Alice Cooper. Their self-released debut album, "Heaven Or Hollywood" had sold over 10,000 copies, and most importantly for me, it had a naked woman's crotch on the cover. Did I mention she was holding a straight razor? I immediately knew this was the band for me. They had gotten great reviews in the UK rock mag "Kerrang," which was like the bible for us hard rockers back in the day. I answered their ad in the local music paper and got the job. Finally getting my chance at actual rock stardom made the lengthy trek back and forth from Syracuse to Rochester for rehearsals palatable. And touring the East Coast in a renovated, spray-paint covered school bus with bunks made from 2x4's and plywood was a dream come true for a rocker bound and determined to pay his dues. There was a lot of substance abuse on that wild road trip but I dimly recall watching our lead singer and guitar player get into a fist fight on the grimy floor of that old bus after a particularly crazy show in Michigan. Or was it Minnesota?

Highlights of the tour included opening for Suicidal Tendencies in Miami and meeting the bass player from Voi Vod in Montreal. Lowlights included getting paid $20 by a club owner to NOT play a show in Lexington, Kentucky and waking up hungover in a sweltering hot Florida parking lot only to discover the only thing to eat on that bus was a wilted head of lettuce floating in a cooler full of melted ice and stale beer. I have no idea how an actual vegetable made it onto our tour bus, as healthy eating was definitely not a priority for us. At least there was mustard to put on the soggy brown leaves as I ate them dejectedly. Like AC/DC prophetically sang, "It's a long way to the top if you wanna rock n roll." Hell, it's a long way to the middle, as my buddy Gordon would say. Uncle Sam recorded one album while I was in the band, 1990's "Letters From London," that got good reviews but didn't sell for shit. Music website Teamrock.com said, "Uncle Sam sounds like what might happen if some Victorian English dandy in a monocle and top hat joined a blood-guzzling garage band from Detroit." That pretty much summed it up for me. I loved being in the band, but Uncle Sam would be my last shot at becoming a rock star. I had been working my ass off to make it in the music business playing the drums to no avail. It wasn't a total loss, because I had a whole lot of fun on the way. But now I had a new dream to chase. A dream filled with travel and duct tape. Moving forward I was fully in roadie mode. I was ready to go all in.

3 MASTERS OF REALITY

The Masters of Reality were the biggest rock band in Syracuse. They were also the weirdest, and the best band in town, all at the same time. They had started out as a sort of gloom and doom synth duo with a cheesy drum machine, but over time they had morphed into a gothic Led Zeppelin-style rock 'n' roll juggernaut.

Have you ever been to a concert that changed your life? The Masters of Reality did that to me every time they played. Their stage show was equal parts rock 'n' roll riot and mind altering acid trip complete with hallucinations. To say they were very theatrical would be an understatement, with a stage show that featured fog machines, light shows, hippie incense burners billowing smoke, and a sound that could wake the dead... or kill you on the spot, depending on your constitution. Imagine a big bald guy in a trench coat, dark eyes burning into your soul, with this amazing baritone voice that hypnotizes you into revealing your deepest darkest secrets...that was Chris, their lead singer. He kind of looked like the guy you'd hate to see hanging around your neighborhood in a beat-up creeper van, but man, could he sing his ass off. The shows were packed with their rather offbeat fans, a crazy blend of punks, goths, rockers, hippies and general weirdos, which Syracuse was full of. Don't forget the guy who always came in an elaborate Grim Reaper costume complete with a creepy mask with battery operated glowing red eyes.

The Masters were one of the few bands in my home town to attract any sort of major label record company interest. This was before the Internet, so bands needed a record deal to get their music out there in any sort of meaningful way. You couldn't post your recordings on YouTube or Bandcamp and get instant access to millions of people. The Masters had to do it the old fashioned way: making demos, showcasing in New York City and sending cassette tapes to record companies and managers.

Getting to roadie for the Masters when they went out of town to do shows was the best. The coolest gig I did with them during that time was in NYC. Somehow they got invited to open up for a prominent Seattle grunge band with an album on top of the charts. It was a pretty awesome opportunity for them and we were all pretty stoked to be in on it. Riding from Syracuse to Manhattan in some unheated panel van full of amps and drums and fog machines might not sound like much fun, but for a rock 'n' roll addict like me it was better than a limo. Squeezed into the cargo hold with me was Shane Preston, the band's lighting guy and de facto tour manager on account of he had the loudest voice of anyone on the road crew, along with Scott the soundman, and Chris Paisley the guitar tech. Once we got loaded in, Shane sent me and Vinnie the drummer to go get the drink tickets for our group from the club owner. Vinnie was an amazing drummer, an old school skinsman who could play anything - jazz, rock, funk, blues...you name it, this guy could make it swing. He joined the band when they left behind their drum machine phase and turned firmly in the direction of rock.

Vinnie and I found the club owner and asked him for the drink tickets for Masters Of Reality.

"How many people are with you guys?" he asked. There were five guys in the band, plus the four roadies. "Nine." He counted out the drink tickets. "Okay, three per person, that makes 27," and handed them over. Vinnie pulled me aside as we headed back to the band's dressing room. "Hang on," he said. "I have an idea". He divided up the tickets. "Okay, how's this? five for me, four for you, and two each for everybody else." I didn't argue. As we continued back to the dressing room with our ill-gotten gains, Vinnie rolled his eyes and sighed theatrically, "I'm so petty and pedestrian."

We curtained off the stage with this big tarp across the front before the show started. The Masters were very theatrical and we really wanted to knock 'em dead here in the Big City. As the band took the stage behind the curtain, the smoke machine began spewing clouds of fog and the intro tape started playing. At a prearranged cue Chris and I would yank the curtain down revealing the band in all their glory just as they began rocking their first song. It was going to look like a million bucks. Think Cheap Trick at Budokan, only cooler. And with a bald guy in a trench coat.

Chris and I crouched down behind the curtain, waiting for the signal. When it came I reached up, yanked down my side of the curtain and scurried off the stage. I looked back, to see how awesome the effect had turned out. There was Chris Paisley, hanging from the stage curtain. Apparently his side of the curtain had been anchored a bit too tightly and wouldn’t come down. He was just sort of dangling there, suspended as the band tore into their opening song. Finally, the curtain gave way, unceremoniously depositing him on the stage in a heap. He crawled off sheepishly.

Midway through the show it was my turn to mess up. Vinnie broke his snare drum, and was calling for me to bring him his spare snare drum. Being too busy getting drinks with all my ill-gotten drink tickets, I had forgotten the spare snare drum out in the van. I had to run out the front door of the club, grab it out of the van, and run it back up to the stage. In the video from the gig, all you can see is this big crowd of people and a snare drum floating above it as I charged through the crowd, holding the drum up over my head. The sea of humanity parted for me and we got the show going again.

The Masters eventually got signed to big record deal with Def American Records and had their debut album produced by Rick Rubin himself. Rubin had produced albums for the Beastie Boys, Slayer, and Run DMC, so it was a big deal. It seemed like a happy ending was in store for the local heroes from Syracuse. But things started to get wonky about this time. The album came out sounding much different from the thunderous post-punk proto-metal sound the Masters had been honing for years. Rubin's production emphasized the traditional, roots rock aspects of their sound while minimizing their dark, progressive side. The self-titled debut album came out sounding suspiciously like a ZZ Top record instead of the goth metal Zeppelin monolith we had been anticipating. Nonetheless, the record got good reviews upon its release and the band hit the road opening for progressive hard rockers King's X. I didn't get to go on the tour. As an unknown opening act on a relatively small tour with no budget, the band took care of most of their own equipment.

The rock 'n' roll road is paved with dreams of glory and success, but in reality there are way more failures. Snatching defeat from the jaws of victory, the Masters of Reality broke up a few weeks into their first big tour. After a show at the Cubby Hole in Chicago, lead singer Chris up and flew home to Los Angeles. Discord and the dreaded "creative differences" teamed up to knock Syracuse's greatest band off their pedestal. The band was in limbo for a while after that. LA based rap label Delicious Vinyl had purchased their recording and publishing contracts and the rights to the debut album from Def American. They re-mastered and re-sequenced the record, added a bonus track and re-released the album with new cover art and a huge media push. Guitarist Tim and Vinnie, the drummer, split off to form their own new band, the Bogeymen, a darker, more progressive sounding outfit than what the Masters had evolved into. They were busily pursuing a record deal while there was still a lot of buzz about the Masters album. I roadied for them at some showcase gigs while they shopped for a new deal. Showcase gigs are when a band hunting for a record deal books a show specifically to get in front of people who can make it happen for them. Usually in a music industry center like New York, Los Angeles or Nashville, the band and their management will pack the guest list with as many record company bigwigs as they can in an effort to impress somebody enough to get a deal. Producers, record company executives, entertainment lawyers, you name it - showcase gigs are usually full to overflowing with music business insiders. Ironically enough, Delicious Vinyl ended up releasing the Bogeymen album. Rock 'n' roll can be an incestuous place.

Meanwhile, Delicious Vinyl wanted the Masters to start touring to promote the re-release, so the band needed a new drummer and guitarist to round out the line-up. They recruited Daniel Rey to play lead guitar. It was a great choice. In contrast to the original guitarist's over the top shredding, Daniel gave the band a more roots rock sound with his bluesy stylings. Rey was well known as a producer having worked on albums by the Ramones, White Zombie and Circus of Power, but he was also an accomplished guitarist having performed with Manitoba's Wild Kingdom. He also played guitar on Joey Ramone's solo album and co-wrote a song with the Ramones.

In a crazy turn of events, the Masters hooked up with British drumming legend Ginger Baker of Cream fame. Talk about a weird combination! They connected through one of Ginger's polo buddies. That's how it happens in California, I guess. They met up to jam and just mess around and ended up hitting it off so well Ginger decided to join the band and do the tour on the spot. Playing on a studio album with the band followed. Stylistically he was worlds apart from what Vinnie had been doing. Ginger's sound was very fluid and almost tribally rhythmic, while Vinnie drove the band harder, in a more straight-ahead rock style. Having Ginger in the band gave the group a lot of publicity, and combined with Delicious Vinyl's marketing push the upcoming tour looked like it was going to be pretty successful.

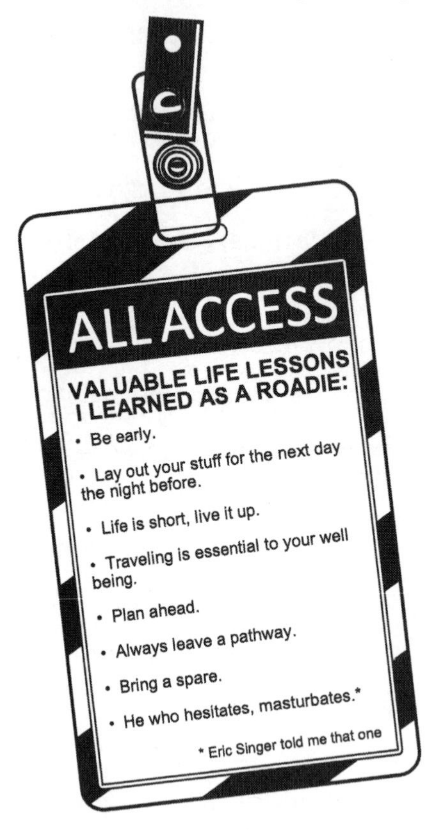

ALL ACCESS
VALUABLE LIFE LESSONS I LEARNED AS A ROADIE:
• Be early.
• Lay out your stuff for the next day the night before.
• Life is short, live it up.
• Traveling is essential to your well being.
• Plan ahead.
• Always leave a pathway.
• Bring a spare.
• He who hesitates, masturbates.*
* Eric Singer told me that one

Getting asked to roadie on their 1990 tour was the starting point for my lifelong dream to finally come true. Of course, I said yes. I had been waiting for this my whole life! My first exposure to the wider world of rock and roll was finally here, and it was a pretty intimidating bunch to be out there with on my first go. I was 24 and didn't really have a clue what I was doing. However, what I lacked in experience I made up for in enthusiasm.

Ginger was a trip to work for. He always had a cigarette of one kind or another hanging out of his mouth, and I'm still not sure that he ever learned my name. He always called me "Young Man", as in "Young Man, where are my drum sticks?" and "Young Man, can I have another Jack and Coke?" He was really cool but we were so different he might as well have been from another planet. It was amazing to watch him play. He had a style that was totally his own, and while I preferred the way Vinnie had played the M.O.R. songs, Ginger's sound really did fit the band's new direction better. He played the only drum solo I ever heard that you could dance to. Ginger's drum set was pretty complex, especially for a neophyte drum tech like me. He had a bunch of little tom toms, and these incredible old cymbals that he told me to never clean. He was an old-school jazz player at heart, and those drummers thought the cymbals sounded better the dirtier they got. If that's true, then these cymbals must have sounded amazing. He still used his ride cymbal and hi-hats from 1968! He had several tiny splash cymbals on these weird looking multi-jointed cymbal stands with all kinds of attachments that were so complicated I was afraid to take them apart because I'd never be able to get them set back up the same way again. So I put them under the bus as is every night in an effort to avoid getting yelled at for setting them up wrong at the next show.

The road crew was Shane, Jeff the guitar tech, Gary the soundman and Kent the tour manager. And me. The. Drum. Roadie. Finally! I was so excited to be doing this I didn't even care what I was getting paid. Which is a good thing, because it was pretty low. But with nothing to compare it to, and considering it was way more than I was making back in Syracuse, I was happy. The tour was a pretty low-budget affair, with the band and crew all sharing on the same bus, with the gear underneath in the luggage bays. It was the most glamorous rock tour I'd ever been on!

The crew guys on this tour were all really cool, which is a necessary skill when you're living on a tour bus together for long periods of time. This being my first tour I had a lot to learn, so a lot of bonehead mistakes were made. I'm eternally grateful that the other guys gave me a chance to figure things out. Gary the sound man was from Los Angeles. He was a veteran of many rock tours, including doing sound for some of my favorite punk bands like X and the Circle Jerks. In fact, the Circle Jerks logo of a slam-dancing punk rocker was modeled after Gary! At least that's what he told me that one time in Topeka while he was drunk.

Jeff the guitar tech was my roommate when we actually got hotel rooms on days off, which wasn't often. Remember, low budget. He had worked for some big-time bands like Heart and Pearl Jam. He was really laid back most of the time and taught me a lot about getting along on the road. High strung and intense is more my style, and he was totally the opposite. I tested his easy-going attitude he first time we roomed together. We had just gotten off the bus after a long overnight drive, and I got in the shower first. Jeff went in after to get cleaned up, only to discover that his inconsiderate roomie had used all the towels! He stuck his dripping wet head out the bathroom door and yelled at me, "Looks like the

Towel Fairy used all the goddamn towels!" and slammed the door. I ran down to the lobby to find him a towel, and believe me, I never towel-hogged again.

We didn't see Kent much except on per diem day and pay day. Per diem (literally Latin for "Per Day"), also known as "PD" is money that is paid to each roadie above and beyond their weekly salary for daily expenses. Best of all, it is given in cash every week. This was before direct deposit was popular, so we also got a paper paycheck every week. This wasn't an ideal fiscal situation for me since I can resist anything but temptation. I ended up cashing most of my checks on the road and spent just about all of my tour pay before I even got back home. Like the actor George Raft famously said, "I spent all my money on booze, broads and fast cars. The rest I just pissed away."

My rock and roll dreams were coming true. The Masters played a lot of college towns with good crowds across the country, and even played a big rock festival at the Boston Garden, which was amazing. I had never even been to Boston and here we were rocking the Garden. But it wasn't all wine and roses. It took a while for Ginger to get used to the Masters theatrical stage presentation. At one show early in the tour, Shane was flooding the stage with fog when he turned on the strobe lights. Ginger freaked out, got lost in all the smoke and lights and couldn't see the drums well enough to hit them! The song ran off the road and went into the ditch, and that was the last time Shane used the strobes around Ginger. Ginger also loved to play games and screw around with me. In the middle of a song he would take his cigarette out of his mouth, toss it in the air, and bat it at me with a drum stick, never missing a beat. I'd have to dodge the burning butts all night. It backfired one night when he missed the cigarette in mid-air and it landed on his floor tom and burned through the plastic drum head. The next time he hit that drum his stick split the damaged head and he got tangled up to his elbow in the broken drum head. Karma is a bitch, old man.

Have you ever been confined to an enclosed space 24 hours a day with a group of people you barely know? Maybe, if you were ever in prison. Or on a tour bus. Sharing a tour bus with the band is a unique experience. Sometimes it works out really well, and sometimes it gets weird. The Masters were more on the weird end of the spectrum, but we all got along well enough. Maybe too well - somebody started anonymously depositing some pretty steamy mash notes in my bunk for a while. Luckily no one tried to get fresh. There's not much room to run on a tour bus.

Soon enough my first tour was over and we headed home. I returned to Syracuse with a new career plan. I was already hooked and wanted more touring.

4 THINGS GET SUICIDAL

What was the next step on my search for ultimate rock 'n' roll glory? Relocating to Los Angeles? Nashville? How about Seattle, where grunge was rapidly conquering the world and the music scene was taking off? Nah, I moved to Tucson, Arizona in 1992 at age 26. Remember Buttzilla, upstate New York's premier grunge-thrash band? Our guitarist Chris transferred from Syracuse University to the University of Arizona a while back, and once established in Arizona, started wooing us with tales of how awesome Tucson was. Don't laugh, Tucson is actually a much cooler place than you might imagine. Back in the early 90's when we moved there the underground music scene was taking off, with a host of great bands and plenty of clubs, venues and record stores all supporting the scene. Chris told us about the Downtown Performance Center, aka the D.P.C., which served as a sort of headquarters for all things cool in Tucson. They had an all-ages live music venue, art space, a recording facility and a variety of other amazing shit happening. The independent record label Toxic Shock records was based in Tucson as well, and Buttzilla dreamed of getting to put out an album with them. The label had released records by bands like Corrosion of Conformity, Raw Power and Skin Yard, all big influences of ours. Motivated to escape the ice and snow, as well as leaving behind some of the burned bridges accumulated during my decade of rock 'n' roll dues-paying in upstate New York, Buttzilla and I packed up the van and headed West.

Every rocker needs cash, so a gig doing sound at a local club imaginatively called "The Rock" was quickly procured thanks to some well-timed name dropping. The Rock was a classic dive bar, complete with a tiny stage, spray painted walls and a malfunctioning air conditioning system that guaranteed every show was hotter than hell. It reminded me of the Lost Horizon back home as they hosted tons of national touring bands as well as some great local bands. For me it was the next best thing to paradise as I mixed sound amid clouds of cigarette smoke and hairspray. But my heart longed for a return to the road. That one short tour with the Masters of Reality had shown me exactly what I wanted to do with this life: be a rock 'n' roll roadie, just like in the Motorhead song. Fortune smiled on me when an old buddy from the rock club days in Syracuse phoned out of the blue. Tom Abraham had been on our ragtag crew of boozy misfits at the Lost Horizon, but after escaping Syracuse he had hit the big leagues working with Queensryche and some other big bands and was now the tour manager and soundman for the legendary punk metal band Suicidal Tendencies. When Tom asked if I wanted to come out on the tour, I was on the next flight out of Tucson. This was it. My big chance to make my rock 'n' roll dream of traveling the world happen.

My journey with Suicidal began on Halloween night in Miami, Florida, opening for Megadeth. ST had been touring all summer in Europe so there were no rehearsals before the tour started. Everyone else on the crew was in the groove and ready to go - everyone except me. Talk about a hard first day on the job. But when you're a roadie, first day problems can get a little crazier than forgetting the PIN to operate the photocopier. Things started off fine. Jimmy the drummer came down to the venue early to go over the setup of his drum kit. Besides being a badass drummer he was into competitive mountain biking, which gave him the endurance to pummel his way through Suicidal's thrash metal set list. He was a nice guy whose patience I was about start testing on a regular basis. He had brought a Gibraltar drum hardware rack on this tour which really simplified things. A drum rack is a series of metal tubes that holds all the drums, cymbals and assorted drummer stuff in place. Everything had memory locks and I just had to label a few things and mark the drum rug so I'd be able to replicate the setup moving forward. However, the drum riser was new to me. The drum riser is the raised platform the drum set sits on. I didn't really have much experience with those, so I pretty just much winged it on the setup.

Now for some boring technical mumbo-jumbo. Try to stay with me, as it has bearing on the story of my first day on the job. And how I almost got fired. Drum risers are traditionally 8' x 8', and made of two 4' x 8' panels that go on top of a metal frame. The panels will usually go on the frame with the seam between the two pieces running from the back of the stage to the front, rather than side to side across the stage. The reasoning behind this would soon become clear to me.

Finally, it's show time! Suicidal hits the stage and starts blasting. Things seem to be going okay. The band is tearing it up, the crowd is going crazy, all is well with the world. Then I look down at Jimmy's feet. There is a small gap between the two drum riser decks which runs right behind his bass drum pedals. I assume I missed spotting this earlier in the day. In any case, it's really small, and I don't think it'll be a problem. But as the show goes on, the gap widens. Jimmy notices, and that's when things get bad. Turns out I've set the riser up in such a way that Jimmy's drum seat is on the upstage riser deck and his bass drum pedals are on the downstage riser deck. So every time he hits the bass drum, which he does about 2,000 times in every song, the front riser deck is pushed away from him. He's essentially pushing the front deck (with most of the drums on it) off the riser frame. As he plays, the drums get further and further away from him with every beat! I'm freaking out, trying to duct tape the thing together which A) doesn't work and B) looks totally stupid, which makes the whole thing worse, if that's even possible.

Gary, the Megadeth production manager, sees disaster looming and comes over to save the day. After a few moments he disappears and comes back with a load strap from one of the trucks. I crawl under the drum riser and we thread the strap under and around the whole riser and cinch it up. It's ugly, there's a big canvas truck strap running along the floor between Jimmy's feet, but at least the drum set is no longer in danger of flying off the front of the stage and into the audience during the show.

Later I found out you normally you get fired for stuff like that.

How did I survive this Day One faux pas? Damned if I know. Maybe since Jimmy was the new guy in the band he didn't have enough stroke to drop the hammer on me, or they just didn't have another good option, or maybe Tom went to bat for me to keep me on the tour. Or maybe Jimmy was just a cool guy and cut me some much-needed slack. The gods of rock 'n' roll continued to bless me, and I survived my first day disaster and started to slowly get my shit together.

After the Suicidal show was over, the KISS show across town was the place to be for any self-respecting rock roadie. God knows there weren't any girls at the Megadeth show. KISS were playing a hockey arena that had been transformed into a huge Halloween party, with fans dressed as the band in their trademark face paint and homemade costumes complete with platform boots.

The rock 'n' roll world is smaller than you think and a bunch of our crew guys knew their crew guys, so we got in free to see the end of the gig and hang out backstage. It was pretty amazing, as all KISS shows are. They had a huge replica of an Egyptian Sphinx head on stage that shot lasers out of its eyeballs. Mix in plenty of explosions, pyro bombs, confetti cannons and flaming columns of smoke and fire, along with a gaggle of drunken Florida girls taking their tops off and you've got a recipe for a good time, rock 'n' roll style.

What a crazy way to end my first day on the job as a real touring roadie. Naturally, we partied like Vikings and somehow made it back to the tour bus where I passed out in my bunk. This would become a pattern.

My fellow roadies for my rookie season of Major League rock 'n' roll touring were guitar techs Bob Acquaviva and Franklin Felder. I already knew Bob from upstate New York where he ran a recording studio in the neighboring town of Utica. He really knew his stuff but more importantly, he was hilarious. It was great having him out there on my first tour. Franklin was an established touring tech, having worked for big name groups like Queensryche and Aerosmith. He also worked for Loverboy, who I guess qualify as a big name group too. Kind of. Anyway, we had a blast together, Franklin taught me all the tricks of the trade and Bob kept us all laughing.

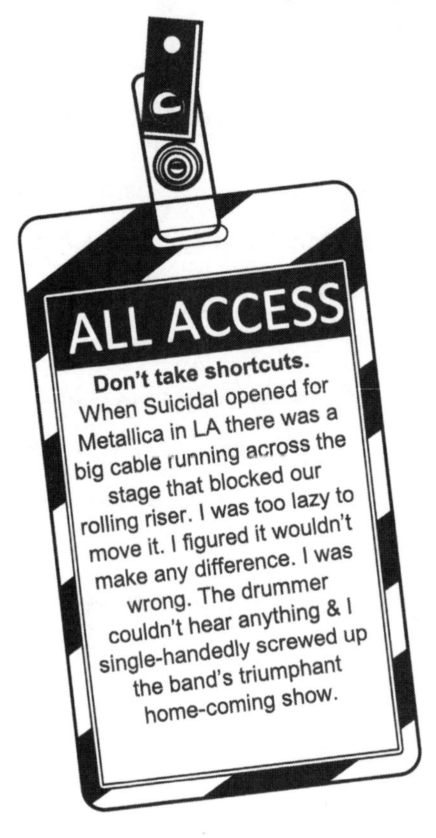

ALL ACCESS
Don't take shortcuts.
When Suicidal opened for Metallica in LA there was a big cable running across the stage that blocked our rolling riser. I was too lazy to move it. I figured it wouldn't make any difference. I was wrong. The drummer couldn't hear anything & I single-handedly screwed up the band's triumphant home-coming show.

Rock 'n' roll was finally paying off. I was now making more money than I had ever made in my life, plus per diems! When I was touring PD ranged from $30 a day up to $75 a day when we were traveling in Japan or other notoriously expensive countries. Of course, at the shows we were fed three meals a day, and hotels on days off were paid for by the tour, so PD was usually spent frivolously. At least that's how I handled it. I would be out there on days off pissing away my money on all sorts of nonsense, as well as copious amounts of alcohol.

Touring on this level was a stark contrast to what I was used to being a part of. Even the Masters Of Reality tour, which had been fairly legit, was more like a string of club dates with an occasional night off in a Motel 6 compared to what I was doing now. On the Megadeth/Suicidal tour we were touring with a full production team, with sound, lighting and stage techs all traveling with the band. We were playing in NHL hockey rinks and NBA basketball arenas across America. We had enough equipment trucks and tour buses to fill a parking lot. On the Masters tour we ate fast food. On this tour there was a dining hall at every show where we had access to catered meals all day. The first time I saw all that free food, to quote my roadie buddy Ken Barr (who you will meet in these pages soon enough), I was like a caveman looking at a rocket ship.

What I liked best about this kind of touring was the idea that all I had to do was roadie. Everything else was taken care of; my meals, lodging, travel, everything was handled by the tour manager and the band's management company. Our days were extremely organized, with a tour itinerary that told us exactly where we were going, what we were doing, and what time it all had to happen. It was kind of like being in the Army, only we got to sleep in.

Feeling like I was in the right place, at the right time, doing exactly what I loved doing was completely new to me. In the "real world" there was so much to balance. Work. Relationships. Money. Rent. Family. On tour there is no such thing as trying to maintain a healthy professional life/personal life relationship. It's all the same. You're out there with your surrogate family making your rock 'n' roll dreams come true 24 hours a day, seven days a week. Your co-workers are also your friends, and your boss has a kick ass drum set you get to play on when he's not looking. I immediately felt like this was where I was meant to be.

The remainder of the Suicidal/Megadeth tour was mostly a blur as I struggled along learning the ropes as a real rock roadie. Mistakes were made. Accidents happened. Hangovers were endured. But by the end of the tour I was sure of one thing; I wanted MORE.

5 THE PLAGUE THAT MAKES YOUR BOOTY MOVE

Suicidal Tendencies were metal heads with hearts of solid funk. Lead singer Mike Muir and ST bassist Robert Trujillo created a side project called Infectious Grooves as an outlet for their love of old school funk and R&B bands. However, Infectious Grooves was no traditional funk band. The band was rounded out by guitarists Adam Siegel from the ferocious punk metal band EXCEL and Dean Pleasants, who played with pop acts like Jessica Simpson as well as funk/R&B artists like George Clinton and Tone Loc. A revolving door of drummers performed with the band, including such greats as Stephen Perkins from Jane's Addiction, Brooks Wackerman of Vandals and Bad Religion fame and studio legend Josh Freese at different times over the years. Infectious had recruited LA drummer Steve Klong as the skinsman for their upcoming tour. Steve had performed with pop stars Wilson Phillips and played on the double-platinum debut Nelson album. Remember those twin brothers with the long blonde hair? They had that huge hit single "Love And Affection" back in 1990? Yeah, me neither.

In 1993 Suicidal Tendencies decided to take Infectious Grooves out on tour as their opening act. They called it the "Busload Of Freaks" tour. I had done one gig with Infectious Grooves before this tour came up. On New Year's Eve 1992, Infectious had played at the Long Beach Arena opening for Stone Temple Pilots. The drummer at that show was Josh

Freese. At the time I didn't know him, and had never worked with him before, but seeing as the gig was a one-off coming at the end of a long Suicidal Tendencies tour I had done with the band, it kind of made sense to have the ST roadies do the show. Josh was really cool, and what an amazing drummer! He went on to become an incredible studio drummer, playing on nearly 400 records including the Suicidal Tendencies "Art Of Rebellion" album. Josh also toured with bands like Nine Inch Nails, Devo, Guns & Roses, and Weezer. Josh played his ass off that night. Literally. He was playing on a rented kit, and about halfway through the Infectious Grooves show his drum throne broke. Between songs he leaned over to me. "Get the spare throne!" I ran off to the drum hardware case and started searching for the spare drum seat. One problem. There was no spare throne! I was able to borrow one from one of the opening bands and we finished the show that way.

The Stone Temple Pilots guys were really nice, considering that they were huge mega rock gods at the time. I hung out with the guitar player Dean for a while shooting the shit and talking music. A year later, in Tokyo while touring with Suicidal Tendencies I was at a record store looking for Japanese bootleg albums when I heard somebody call out, "Hey, J Mann!" I looked around in surprise. There's Dean! Turns out that Stone Temple Pilots was over there touring too. I met the guy once and he remembered me a year later. Just goes to show not all rock stars are assholes.

This "Busload Of Freaks" tour would be especially interesting because Mike and Robert would be performing with both bands on stage every night. This would make for some really long days for the two of them. We found out the roadies would be doing double-duty as well. This was the first ST tour I had been on where they brought out full production. This means we were carrying our own sound and lighting as well as the band's stage gear. This was great news for the bands, as it meant they would have the same gear every night. Things would be much more consistent than if they were using locally provided sound and lights, or "stacks & racks." That is where touring bands carry some sound gear, but the larger items like speaker cabinets and power racks get provided locally. One of the most expensive things on a tour are trucks and drivers, so anything that can be done to reduce the amount of gear you bring (as well as the number of vehicles needed to haul it around) the better. But this time ST was going all in, carrying their own light show, sound system, staging, even wardrobe cases, which seemed weird seeing as they all wore shorts and Suicidal Tendencies tee shirts on stage. Along with the extra gear came extra roadies, and an extra bus for the crew. Bob and Franklin were back for this tour as my partners in roadie crime.

I met Steve Klong at the production rehearsals as the bands and crew prepped everything for the tour. He was a typical drummer, bouncing off the walls with energy, exhibiting borderline bipolar behavior and cracking jokes non-stop. Like I said, a typical drummer. He had these crazy long sideburns that Bobby Savage, our tough-as-nails stage rigger, wanted to shave off the moment he laid eyes on poor

Steve. I was definitely going to have my hands full with this guy, as he was very particular about his gear. I had to let him know I would do my best but with two drummers to take care of on this trip we would all need to work together and stay flexible. Luckily Jimmy, the Suicidal Tendencies drummer, was his usual easy-going self. How somebody could be that good at playing the drums and still be that humble is beyond me.

Infectious Grooves was sort of a concept band. Their album covers featured a cast of outrageous funky lizard-people, featuring their ringleader, a jive-talking zoot-suit wearing reptile named Sarsippius. The Infectious Grooves albums featured little spoken word snippets of Sarsippius speaking, skits with him interacting with the band, criticizing their music, stuff like that. They even released a record titled "Sarsippius' Ark"! It was pretty funny stuff on the albums, but who would have thought they would actually take it to the next level and bring Sarsippius out on tour? They actually had a buddy of theirs who came on the tour to act as Sarsippius the lizard-man in the show. He had an elaborate costume that looked kind of like the Geico gecko disguised as a pimp from a 70's TV cop show. It had a wireless microphone inside the big foam rubber lizard head so Sarsippius could talk during the show. He even sang a song with the band!

One of the most disgusting things ever happened on this tour, after a show at the 9:30 Club in Washington DC. The 9:30 Club is a legendary rock 'n' roll venue, everyone from the Beastie Boys to Black Flag has played there. It moved to a more respectable location in 1996, but when we played there it was still at its original address in the Atlantic building, located in a pretty bad neighborhood in downtown DC. The building didn't have enough power to run our sound and lights, so we had to bring in a generator which was located outside the load in doors in an alley behind the club. The show went off without a hitch, other than having to chase away the hordes of homeless guys who lived in the alley and kept trying to sneak into the show. Everything went great until load out. Our sound tech Stuart was pulling in the feeder cable that runs from the stage to the generator and packing it in the feeder cable trunk. The feeder is an extremely heavy cable, and the only way to haul it in is to create a rhythm where you're almost throwing it in loops into the trunk. Once you get some momentum going you don't want to stop because it is extremely hard to get it moving again. Stuart was hauling in the cable when we heard him abruptly stop and cry out in disgust. "Oh my God!" he wailed. "Who the fuck took a shit on the feeder cable?" Evidently one of the urban outdoorsmen in the alleyway had taken it upon himself to empty his bowels directly on the cable that Stuart had been wrestling with. The poor guy was literally covered in shit. He finished the load out in his underwear after throwing away his soiled clothing.

The shows were a blast and the fans loved getting to see both Suicidal and their infamous side project on one stage. Mike and Robert held up pretty well despite pulling double duty every night. It was just about one short month of ST/IG shows and they were able to rock the socks off the crowd every time.

6 WELCOME TO EUROPE. NOW, GO HOME.

After the Infectious Grooves/Suicidal Tendencies tour ended ST headed to Europe to open for Metallica on their stadium tour. Metallica was touring in support of their huge breakout "Black Album." That's the one with "Enter Sandman," and it had catapulted the band to super-stardom. Metallica had been touring almost continually since the album hit the charts in 1991. This was a great opportunity for Suicidal to play for a ton of metal fans all summer, thanks in part to the fact that Suicidal and Metallica had the same management company, the NYC based Q-Prime Management. Q-Prime was giving ST a tremendous push by putting them out on the road all summer long with the biggest band on the planet.

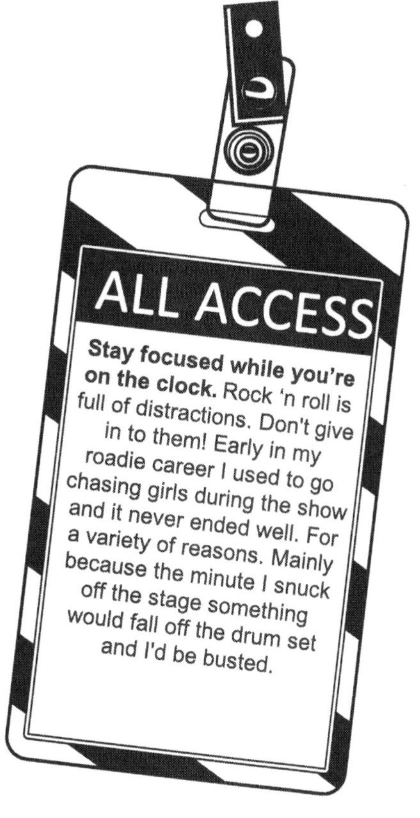

ALL ACCESS
Stay focused while you're on the clock. Rock 'n roll is full of distractions. Don't give in to them! Early in my roadie career I used to go chasing girls during the show and it never ended well. For a variety of reasons. Mainly because the minute I snuck off the stage something would fall off the drum set and I'd be busted.

Finally, Europe! The prospect of traveling overseas combined with opening for Metallica had me pretty excited. That's not quite true - I was going fucking apeshit. I couldn't believe I had gone from doing sound at clubs to touring Europe on a Metallica tour so quickly. There were no crazy drummers wearing motorcycle helmets here. This was the big leagues. It was literally a dream come true.

Europe was a total shock for me. Remember, I was an under-educated hillbilly from the wilds of upstate New York. These days Europe has become somewhat more American-ized, but back in the early 90's it was still a very different place for an Ugly American like me to visit. Businesses all closed on Sundays and there were virtually no 24-hour or late night restaurants. I was flabbergasted when I got to my hotel room upon arriving in Hannover and discovered that there was no place open to eat. At 9pm! I mean absolutely nothing. I ended up eating the potato chips and candy bars in my hotel mini-bar for dinner. At least there was plenty of German beer to wash it down.

Touring with Metallica was an education, like a master class in Advanced Roadie Awesomeness. They had been on the road virtually non-stop for about 30 months by this time, and to say their crew and production team was a well-oiled machine would be a total understatement. 2 ½ years on the road without a break would kill most people. These guys were high level pros, and here was little old me with about three months of touring gigs under my belt. I felt like a runny-nosed little brother trying to keep up with the big kids. The culture shock for me was intense. The first time I ran out on Metallica's stage to start setting up Jimmy's drum set I almost got vertigo and fell down. Everything was so big.

Working on stage in front of thousands and thousands of people is an acquired skill. It's like being in a volcano surrounded by the swirling magma of molten humanity, an endless sea of faces with their eyes on you. You go about your tasks completely exposed. Some people actually enjoy this invasive scrutiny, most notably narcissistic sociopaths - or "lead singers" as they are most frequently referred to.

Speed was also of the essence in this new environment. Getting on and off the stage quickly in order to keep the tour production on schedule was critical, and there was no deviating from the Metallica timetable. Working with this group, I learned to keep my head down, my mouth shut, and just do my gig. I was able to get a handle on things once I rationalized that the drum riser was the same size in the little clubs we were playing with Infectious Grooves as it was in the Olympic Stadium in Berlin with Metallica: 8 feet by 8 feet. Focusing in on that reality helped a lot and soon I got my act together, started having some fun and enjoying things a bit more.

Then Suicidal's lead vocalist Mike asked me to introduce the band at the beginning of each show. Perhaps he figured out I had the biggest mouth of anybody on the crew, making me a natural choice for the job. Either way, it was another dream coming true for our hero. The intro tape would be playing, the crowd going crazy, the band gathered around ready to hit the stage, and Mike would hand me the microphone. Amped up on pure adrenaline, I would try to come up with something cool to say, but usually I would just roar, "Alright, Berlin (or wherever we were playing that day)! Are you ready for the motherfucking hate? Please welcome SUICIDAL TENDENCIES!" Poetry it ain't, but the band certainly seemed to like it.

At the time I didn't know if I'd ever make it back to Europe so I became a voracious sight-seer and did a lot of exploring on days off. Exploring the bars near our hotel with the other guys on the road crew? Definitely. Mixing in some cultural experiences was a priority as well. Notre Dame, the Shroud of Turin, the Eiffel Tower, and that world-famous international cultural center, The Bulldog hash bar in Amsterdam were all on my itinerary during my maiden voyage through Europe. Not bad for a kid from upstate New York who barely managed to get a high school degree. Luckily I also had a relentless will to rock, and that was finally starting to pay off.

In addition to the Metallica shows, Suicidal were also playing headlining gigs, playing at festivals and opening yet even more stadium shows, this time for Guns N' Roses. Being on tour with the two biggest rock 'n' roll bands in existence was not a bad way for a rock 'n' roll junkie like me to spend his summer vacation. The Guns N' Roses tour was more laid back compared to the clockwork precision of the Metallica tour, but everyone on the GNR tour lived in fear of the lead singer, Axl Rose. We were advised to steer clear of him, which was pretty easy to do. Axl wasn't around much except when it was show time for the Guns, and even then he had a phalanx of security guys and handlers accompanying him. I would have had a hard time getting near the guy even if I had wanted to. And common sense dictates that you stay away from anyone in a kilt and body armor. The other band guys from Guns N' Roses were much easier to deal with and treated us cool. I even made friends with their drum tech, who was also from upstate New York. He would let me hang out in this secret little room he had built under the stage where Matt, the GNR drummer, would chill out during the guitar solos and bass solos and Axl's harmonica solo or whatever. The band had a tattoo artist traveling on tour with them in case anybody wanted to get some new ink, and a party planner whose only job was to coordinate their after-show-parties. No, really. He would create different themes, rent decorations, hire caterers, book famous DJs and invite celebrities. These guys knew how to live.

Suicidal Tendencies played one of the craziest shows ever on this tour: July 4, 1993 in Toulouse, France, at a little rock club called Le Bikini. I was 27 years old. The club was nice, although small, with a smooth concrete stage. They even had a swimming pool out back for the bands and roadies to use. We celebrated Independence Day out there before the show, American style, with beers and whatever passes for hot dogs in France. I'm pretty sure there was some sort of goose liver involved. The club owner gave our tour manager the good news that the show was sold out, and there was going to be a big crowd there to see Suicidal.

Now, if there's one thing French people like to do, it's smoke. And if there's one thing promoters like to do, it's sell tickets. As the crowd started coming in we could see that this little club was going to be packed to the walls. As we tuned the guitars and got the stage ready for the band the fans kept pouring in. It soon became clear that the promoter had oversold the show in order to make as much money as possible. I don't know if they have fire codes or occupancy limits but this place was definitely jammed past capacity. We had water and towels in case the band got too hot on stage, and ST was used to playing small venues when they had to, so we figured we'd be okay.

I introduced the band and they hit the stage. The crowd went bananas from the first note and everything seemed to be going great. Suicidal was enjoying a lot of popularity in France with their new record and the crowd was totally into it. As the band kept playing, the crowd kept smoking and the temperature kept rising. Jimmy the drummer was sweating like crazy and I was running out of towels for him. The humidity in the club got so high, condensation began forming on the cement stage. Mike the singer loves to run around on stage during the show to pump up the crowd, but tonight he was sliding around like he was wearing ice skates.

Jim George was the ST production manager for that tour and he came up with a bunch of extra towels and a big bucket of ice from somewhere. The guitar roadies would run out between songs and try to dry off a place for Mike to do his thing. It would last a few minutes then the whole stage would be slick as ice again. The guitars were getting too wet to tune properly. Up on his drum riser near the blazing stage lights Jimmy was really suffering. It was so hot, and there was no ventilation at the back of that little stage where we were. I started soaking towels in ice water and draping them over his back. When the ice cold towels hit his body steam would start coming off him. It was insane. Sweat was just pouring out of him like a faucet. Luckily, Jimmy was in great shape from all that mountain biking so he was strong enough to get through it.

The big concern for the crew was that Mike or one of the guitar players was going to take a bad fall on that slick concrete stage and get themselves seriously injured. It was our job to try to keep the guys safe and able to do their thing.

Imagine a blender filled with sweaty French metal heads. The kids were going crazy, slam-dancing, headbanging, jumping off the stage - all while smoking unfiltered French cigarettes. Somehow the band made it through the set and said goodnight to the crowd. As the fans filed out the band guys ran out the back door and jumped straight into that swimming pool to try and rehydrate. Happy Independence Day, Toulouse!

7 EUROPEAN ROCK FESTIVALS ARE A GREAT WAY TO MAKE FRIENDS

One of the coolest parts about touring in Europe was the summer festival season. In Europe the big concert promoters put together these huge three or four day long festival events with 20 - 30 bands playing each day. Hundreds of thousands of people show up, and there's camping, vendor villages where you can buy stuff, food shops making all kinds of tasty things to eat, people having sex in the forest, beer gardens, it's like heaven on earth for any self-respecting rock fan. And the bands are amazing. The promoters tend to mix up the styles each day, so rather than just putting 20 speed metal bands on the bill they frequently put lots of other musical genres in there too to shake things up and keep it interesting.

For example, the Hamburg Rocks festival in 1993 had Suicidal Tendencies, Anthrax and Rage Against The Machine playing, which all fit snugly into the heavy metal genre. But Iggy Pop (the godfather of punk rock), Living Colour (funky guitar hero rock) and the Levellers (political punkers) were also on the bill. That was a great show and a cool mix of styles. Seeing Rage Against The Machine was amazing. At another festival - the SuperBang '94 Festival in Germany - the lineup was Midnight Oil, Suicidal Tendencies, Public Enemy, Rollins Band, Helmet, Frank Black and Red Hot Chili Peppers. Everything from the angsty rage-ranting of Henry Rollins to Hip Hop to post-punk. It was so cool to see all those different kinds of bands on one stage, and they all killed it.

The big European festivals were also kind of like Roadie Summer Camp: a great chance to get to see some old tour buddies backstage. You were almost certain to run into at least one or two people you had worked with previously at these big festival gatherings. One of the main rules of the roadie world is to never pass up an opportunity to have a beer or three with some old friends.

One thing that kind of sucks about these festival gigs is that there are so many bands the logistics can get completely crazy. Everything is on an incredibly rigid time schedule. If you aren't on top of things you can miss your time slot to get loaded out and then you're stuck there for hours and hours until the next opportunity to get your truck in the loading dock and escape. Or if you miss your soundcheck time, you're screwed. No soundcheck for you! Or if you can't get another band on the bill to move their stuff to make room for you, life can get really hard. Later in my roadie career, when Alice Cooper was playing this big European festival with Status Quo, our stage crew was getting pushed around by the Quo guys big time. They were these salty old Brits and they weren't cutting us any slack whatsoever. We had no room for our stuff on the sides of the stage, they didn't want to move their drums, we were just getting walked all over. I came up with the idea that we should just wear toilet seats around our necks instead of backstage passes if we were going to get shit on like this. Somehow this idea never caught on with my fellow roadies.

Usually the other crews were easy to work with and everybody pulled together to make things run smoothly. I mean, we're all in this together, right? Like when Alice Cooper was playing the Loreley festival in Germany. We were playing right before Meat Loaf. That's right, the voice behind those iconic rock classics like Paradise By The Dashboard Light and Bat Out Of Hell. The meat man himself! He was in the Rocky Horror Picture Show, for cryin' out loud! Alice and the band are up there doing their thing, chopping heads off, stabbing people with swords, the usual. All of a sudden our drummer breaks his bass drum head. Now there are two things you can't do without on a drum set. One is the snare drum, the other is the bass drum. Now, we had plenty of spare snare drums, but we hadn't brought a spare bass drum out on this tour, just extra bass drum heads. Normally the bass drum head never breaks. Ever. In 10 years on the road I saw it happen once. This time. To me. So I run out there on stage in front of a sold-out festival crowd and start fixing it. The only way to do this is to drag the kick drum out on stage and start taking the broken head off to change it out for a fresh one. First I have to disconnect the bass drum pedal. Then loosen each screw holding the head on. There's only so fast you can do this stuff, and it's taking forever. I can see Alice Cooper literally standing on the side of the stage glaring at me and tapping his foot impatiently. Suddenly the drum roadie for Meat Loaf comes running out carrying Meat Loaf's bass drum. "Dude! Here!" He hands it to me. It didn't match our drum set, and it was a different size, but in that situation beggars can't be choosers. We stick it in place, put the pedal back on, and the band starts playing again and finishes the show. That guy saved my ass.

Meeting rock legends at these big festivals is the best part of the whole thing, sometimes in unconventional ways. At one big festival, I was taking a leak backstage when someone came in and started using the urinal next to me. I glanced over, then did a double take. It was Ian Astbury! From The Cult! I'm a huge Cult fan! Their "Electric" album was my perfect drinking soundtrack for much of the 90's. Trying to play it cool wasn't working and I couldn't help myself from looking over at him a few times while we urinated together. We even made eye contact. Okay, so he probably thought I was trying to peek at his junk, but it was really just me being a starstruck rocker saying hello to one of my rock 'n' roll heroes in my own special way.

At the Dynamo Festival in Eindhoven, Netherlands, I was watching the bands play from the side of the stage after we were done loading the truck and waiting to leave. The guy standing next to me offered me a hit from a bottle of Jack Daniels. A real rock roadie never turns down a drink, so we started shooting the shit and sharing the bottle. After the band onstage was finished my new friend said, "Okay man, nice to meet you. I gotta go play." Turns out it was the guitar player from Monster Magnet. Nice guy.

Those meetings were all a lot of fun. But the greatest rock star encounter of my life happened on tour with Megadeth at the "Gods Of Metal" festival in Milan, Italy in 2001. This was an all-star heavy metal music festival with tons of kick ass bands like Judas Priest, Savatage and Motorhead. At these big hairy heavy metal festivals there are usually several rolling drum risers on wheels backstage to coordinate faster set changes and keep the whole production moving and on time. You set up your drums on one of these rolling platforms and when it's your turn to play they push the whole thing out on stage, plug in the microphones and off you go. On this occasion I had to crawl under Jimmy's drum riser to fix something. As I was crawling out from under I came face to face with a pair of dusty white cowboy boots. I looked up. There before me stood Lemmy from Motorhead. It was like looking up and seeing God. The clouds parted. A choir of angels played "Ace Of Spades" on their golden trumpets. Lemmy was wearing tattered denim shorts, a beat-to-shit leather biker jacket and a black cowboy hat. He grinned down at me. "Where did you come from?" he growled in that famous Lemmy-voice that sounds just like all the Motorhead records you're ever listened to, except better because he's actually

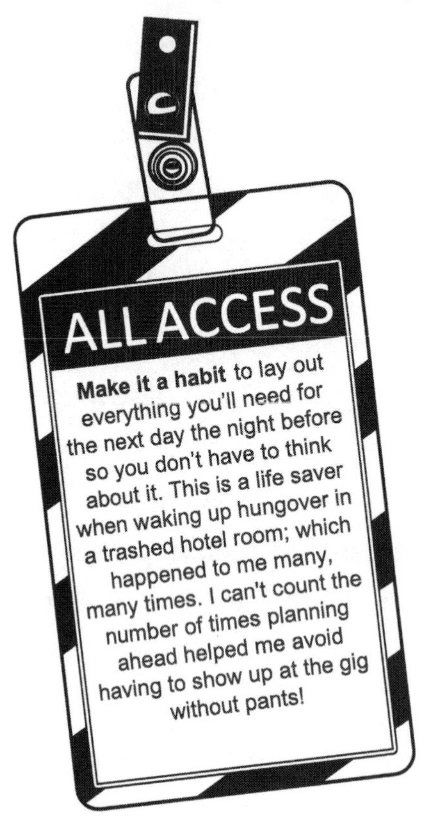
ALL ACCESS
Make it a habit to lay out everything you'll need for the next day the night before so you don't have to think about it. This is a life saver when waking up hungover in a trashed hotel room; which happened to me many, many times. I can't count the number of times planning ahead helped me avoid having to show up at the gig without pants!

talking to YOU now. He was an awe-inspiring sight in those short shorts, especially from that angle. He reached down and gave me a hand up. I swore to never wash that hand again. But then I figured I'd probably better go wash it right away. During a few drinks with him and the rest of the gang after the show it turned out he was the nicest, funniest guy you'd ever want to meet. Lemmy was one of the many great rock 'n' rollers that passed away in 2016. What a tough year that was. So glad I got to bump into him at least once.

One person I dreamed of meeting at one of the big festivals but couldn't get within a thousand yards of was Ozzy Osbourne. In 1995 Alice Cooper was playing with Ozzy at the "Monsters Of Rock" festival in Sao Paulo, Brazil. Who was geeking out at the prospect of working a gig with the almighty Ozz man? This guy! As a huge Black Sabbath fan for a lifetime (remember, the very first song we learned in my very first rock 'n' roll band was "Iron Man"?) I was dying for the chance to meet Ozzy. Normally I don't go into fanboy mode when I am out working on tour, but this is fucking OZZY OSBOURNE, man!

Turns out Ozzy has a small army of handlers whose main purpose is to keep him away from everybody and make sure he can find his way to the stage. Seriously. They had rope lights all over the backstage area from the dressing room to the stage to guide the Ozz-man from place to place. It was like he was an airplane coming in for a landing. "Just stay between the lines Ozzy, the stage is dead ahead, you can't miss it!" Ozzy seemed like a nice enough guy, from what I could tell from afar, and it was a real drag to miss the chance to tell him how much his music had meant to me over the years. I'm sure he hears that shit all the time, though.

8 I COME FROM A LAND DOWN UNDER

Fresh new lands were now ready to conquer. Traveling the world with a rock 'n' roll band was already making my wildest dreams come true when a new destination beckoned from across the sea - Australia! In October of 1993, Suicidal Tendencies got invited to open for Alice In Chains on their Australian tour. This was a tremendous gig for the band, as Alice in Chains was on top of the rock world at that point. They were touring to support their latest album *Dirt*, which had debuted at number six on the Billboard charts, and eventually sold over four million copies. Australia? Multi-Platinum rock stars? Yes please! This whole roadie thing was working out better than I could have ever imagined.

Alice in Chains was pulling in big crowds and playing big rooms. On top of that, the Alice In Chains guys were big Suicidal Tendencies fans so they made sure their roadie crew gave us just about everything we needed. The only downside for me was that because of the size of the stages we were playing on, I would have to set up Suicidal's drums for sound check, then break them down and move them off the stage so the first band would have room to play. The first band on the tour was the Poor Boys, who were a great Australian band featuring the younger brother of Angus and Malcolm Young (of AC/DC fame) on guitar. Australia actually had a law that an Australian band had to perform on the bill at any concert, which was great for the Poor Boys but made my day a little tougher. You see, once the Poor Boys were done opening the show, I would have to wait for them to clear the stage, hustle Jimmy's drum set back out on stage, and get it all set back up so ST could play. Normally once the drums are set up they stay put until after we play. This made a bit of extra work for me, which I unwisely complained about in front of the Alice In Chains production manager early in the tour. He made it clear that my pissing and moaning wasn't going to be tolerated.

"What's that? You have to take down a drum set and set it back up again? That sucks. Hey, what do you do for a living again?"

In my defense, it was a pretty big drum set. Anyhow, I quit my bitching after that. I was having so much fun in Australia I really didn't have anything to complain about. Australia is an amazing place, and we even had some days off here and there to check it out. The country is beautiful, and the people were really friendly to Americans there, especially the women. Apparently Australian guys have a reputation for being jerks, so the Australian girls were very motivated to see if American guys were any better. We did our best to represent our homeland with honor and distinction. Australia had many exciting new beers to try, and crazy foods like a McDonald's Big Mac loaded with beets and a fried egg. Now that's a guaranteed hangover cure. After spending the summer touring Europe it was also kind of nice to be back where I could understand the language. The shows were doing great, mostly sold out, so the band was happy and everybody was having a good time.

On a day off in Melbourne our guitar tech Dave Lee and I went to a wildlife park to see the exotic local animals. Taking a shuttle bus from our hotel to the wildlife park, we got there early and grabbed two seats in the back, where the cool kids sit. As the bus started to fill up, two things became apparent. First, we were the only white people on the bus. Second, the bus was totally full - it was completely packed with Japanese tourists, except for me and Dave. As soon as the bus pulled into the zoo parking lot Dave leaped out of his seat and stampeded down the aisle toward the exit. Now, Dave was a big dude. He's really gotten in shape in recent years and looks great (good on ya, Dave), but in 1993 seeing this XXL guitar roadie coming at you at high speed was an awe-inspiring sight. There was an audible gasp from our fellow passengers. Dave called back over his shoulder as the bus came to a stop, still sprinting for the door, "Hurry up J. Mann! We gotta beat these fuckers to the zoo!" The bus doors hissed open just as Dave hit the exit. Perfect timing. He leapt off the bus with his long hair streaming behind him and headed for the ticket window. By the time I caught up with him he had our tickets and we got into the zoo ahead of all the other passengers. Turns out Dave hates waiting in line, and the prospect of being in line behind all those people to get into the zoo was too much for him to bear.

The wildlife park was amazing, beautifully landscaped and stocked with a wide variety of native Australian flora and fauna as well as other exotic animals. We bumped into a couple of the Suicidal Tendencies band guys, but went our separate ways after saying hello. When you spend 24 hours a day with your boss you don't really want to hang out together on your day off.

The park had a place where, for a fee, you could actually hold a live koala bear. With your own hands! We were both excited to try it. Unfortunately for Dave, there was a long line of folks waiting to cuddle a koala. Once we got there we were both looking forward to actually holding a real live koala bear, the symbol of Australia. They're practically the Australian National Bird, for crying out loud!. It'd be like holding a Bald Eagle in America. This was going to be great.

Turns out koala bears are mean little bastards. They're plant-eaters, but evolution equipped them with some badass defense mechanisms including razor sharp claws and a nasty attitude. So nasty, in fact, that you can't actually "hold" a koala. Unless you want to get the shit scratched out of you. They have the koala latch onto a koala-colored pillow with those pointy little claws and you hold the pillow. Luckily their teeth are designed specifically for eating eucalyptus leaves, so that end is fairly safe. Dave was bummed about not getting to really hold one, but we did get some great pictures with the little pillow-clutching beasts before giving them back to the koala wranglers.

Dave and I also go to go see the "fairy penguins" on Phillip Island. Australia is home to the smallest species of penguins on Earth. They max out at about twelve inches tall.

They live in sandy burrows on the beach, and head out in the morning to swim in the ocean, eat fish, and do important penguin things all day. At night they all come back at once and walk together up the beach to their burrows. They do this as a group for protection from predators, an evolutionary safety in numbers thing. There can be hundreds of them marching up the beach from the water at once. Yes, it's unbelievably cute, and as a result buses full of tourists arrive at the beach nightly to see the parade. Dave and I went to check it out and it was amazing. Sadly there was no option to hold a fairy penguin for a picture. The little guys are protected by some pretty strict laws, and there are even volunteer groups that patrol the beaches to protect them from predators. I even heard there was a particularly zealous penguin advocate who was shooting foxes, dogs and cats if they were caught preying on the birds. Talk about being all in for your cause!

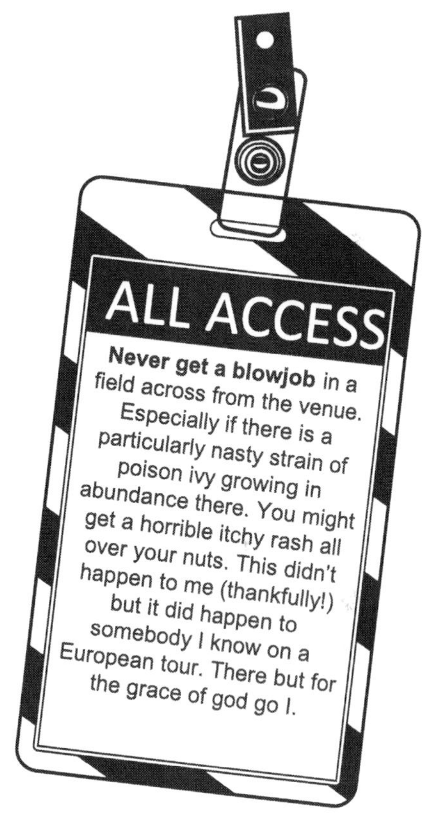

ALL ACCESS
Never get a blowjob in a field across from the venue. Especially if there is a particularly nasty strain of poison ivy growing in abundance there. You might get a horrible itchy rash all over your nuts. This didn't happen to me (thankfully!) but it did happen to somebody I know on a European tour. There but for the grace of god go I.

Between our wildlife adventures we managed to squeeze in a few rock 'n' roll shows, too. The vibe on this tour was great. The Alice in Chains band and crew were all nice guys, but Layne, the singer, was especially cool. Most lead singers in a band that's selling four million albums have a crappy attitude, not to mention an assistant, or a wrangler, or a security guy, or something similar with them at all times when they're on tour. Handlers, you know. Not Layne. We would find him hanging out by the pool by himself at the hotel on a day off, or we'd spot him passing through the lobby on his way out of the hotel, flying solo. He just kind of went under the radar like that. He was always really easy to get along with. Looking back, we now know he had a drug problem. In 1993 it was already getting bad. The band couldn't tour as much as they wanted to because of it, and Layne eventually died from a drug overdose in 2002. Was that why he didn't have the usual rock star trappings, like security escorts and personal assistants with him when he went out? So he could get away to do his own thing? I don't know. I do know he was a super cool guy, a great singer and frontman and it's a goddamn shame that he ended up the way he did. What a heart-breaking waste of talent.

So the girls were friendly, the animals were amazing, the people were cool despite making some questionable life choices, and the shows were going great. Then things got weird.

After Suicidal finished their set in Melbourne, the Alice in Chains production manager came running up to me looking a little freaked out.

"Don't take those drums down yet!" he said, then took off backstage. This was understandably confusing. Normally after the opening band is done the headliner's crew wants us to get our stuff off the deck as soon as possible. Then our tour manager gave us the news. Sean, the drummer for Alice in Chains, had gotten hurt and wasn't going to be able to perform that night. Right there, on the spot they asked the Suicidal Tendencies drummer Jimmy if he could fill in... Jimmy didn't think twice and said, "Hell yes!" Now, Jimmy's a total badass, but this took some balls. He literally had about 30 minutes notice before getting on stage with one of the biggest bands in the world at a sold-out show. Jimmy's played with a million bands, he plays all styles, reads music, the whole thing. He got up there on Sean's drum set and just nailed it. Crushed it. Knocked it out of the park. A few of the endings were a little wonky, but you'd never have known it was someone else up there on drums if they hadn't told the crowd. Jimmy ended up doing the rest of the tour drumming with Alice in Chains AND Suicidal, pulling double-duty every night for about three or four shows. After a few soundcheck rehearsals with those guys they were really tight and sounding great. I expect he got compensated nicely, too. He earned it, that's for sure.

We never found out exactly what happened with Sean. I had heard he got hurt skateboarding around Melbourne or something, but another rumor went around that he had actually hurt himself trashing his drum set at the end of the show the night before. Not sure what the real story is.

Sadly, there are only so many places to play in Australia and eventually we had to leave. Good bye, fairy penguins. You will not be forgotten.

9 TOURING WITH METALLICA (AGAIN, SOME MORE)

After the Suicidal tour ended it was once again back to Tucson to wait for ST to go back on the road. They had no tour dates booked until the summer, so dire financial conditions forced me to find other temporary employment. I found a few gigs doing sound at clubs in town and even took a job flipping burgers to make ends meet. I had been making decent money on the last tour, but I certainly hadn't saved any of it. I guess I figured there would always be another tour coming along, so I never saved any of the money I made on tour until much later in my roadie career. Anyway, I somehow made it to June by subsisting on a strict diet of ramen noodles and cheap beer. Finally, back on the road!

After spending most of 1993 opening for Metallica, Guns & Roses and Alice In Chains, this year Suicidal Tendencies was once again headed back out on tour with Metallica, this time in the United States and Canada. It seemed like their management guys at Q-Prime were making a serious effort to catapult the band into the big time by getting them out in front of as many metal fans as possible as Metallica's opening act on all these huge tours. The band was also releasing a new album, cheerfully titled "Suicidal For Life." It would be their first with the current lineup and was expected to make or break the band.

The first gig of the tour was in Buffalo, NY. It was most of the same Metallica crew guys from last year. Their production manager this tour was a big, imposing fellow named Dan Braun who intimidated the hell out of me. I spent most of my time on this tour just trying to stay out of his way and off his shit list, which was kind of hard when you're a young, inexperienced screw-up like me. The Suicidal backline crew was me, Dave Lee, and Billy Bush. I had a horrible habit during my first few tours of getting completely, totally, abysmally blackout drunk the night before the first show. I think I was so happy to be back out on tour that I always ended up celebrating with my roadie bros way too hard. As a result, I was usually in terrible shape on the first day of the tour, which when you're the opening band as we were here, is basically the most important day of the entire tour. They say you never get a second chance to make first impression, and sadly, my first impressions were usually that of a hungover disphit mumbling incoherently between trips to the bathroom to throw up. It's a wonder I lasted ten years in the business, but I was somehow able to survive myself long enough to get my act together...eventually. When the new Suicidal album came out there was a box of new CDs on the bus. I was interested to check it out. The band was performing several songs from this newest release in the live show, so I had heard them plenty of times, but I was interested in hearing how they came across on the recording versus the over-the-top intensity of the live versions.

The album sounded great. I was keyed into the drum sounds especially, but the whole tone of the record captured the band's essence perfectly. The songs were intense and angry yet somehow melodic, but always maintaining that bone-crushing heaviness. The only problem I could find was that there wasn't a single song that could possibly get played on MTV or the radio. Remember, this was before YouTube or streaming music services like Spotify. Bands still depended on radio and TV to get their music out in front of people. But it seemed like every song on the new album was absolutely loaded with obscenities. It was almost like they were intentionally trying to make an album that nobody could play on the air. Even if you tried to edit out the curse words it would just be one long "beep". The song titles will give you an idea of what I'm talking about... "Don't Give A Fuck", "No Fuckin' Problem", "Suicyco MuthaFucka", "No Bullshit", and "Fucked Up Just Right" to name a few. Are you seeing a trend? One night we actually sat down with a pen and paper and tried to count all the F bombs on the album. We ran out of paper. It was crazy. The album made it to #82 on the Billboard charts but fell off after three weeks and never made much commercial impact for the band. Too bad because that record kicked ass.

After one memorable show on that Metallica tour I was back in the Suicidal Tendencies dressing room getting something to eat. The Suicidal guys were pretty cool about letting us roadies have access to their dressing room and the food & drinks provided for the band, especially when we were all sharing a tour bus. After the shows we would pack up any leftover stuff in the dressing room and cart it out to the tour bus for that night's drive. Sometimes when there are separate band and crew buses the vibe can be a bit more divided, but on this tour we were one big mostly-happy family.

So I was back there grabbing a sandwich when I realize it's almost time for Metallica to go onstage. I head for the door when suddenly I hear Metallica's singer James warming up in the hallway right outside our dressing room door. He does this vocal warmup thing right before they go onstage so he sounds good right off the bat on the first song. Aw crap, now I'm trapped in here. I don't want to bust in on Metallica while they are about to go on stage, so I figure I'll wait till they leave then head out to check out their show.

Then the door suddenly bangs open and Metallica's drummer Lars bursts into our dressing room. "Hey man!" he says to me, drumsticks in hand. "How was your show?" He's amped up and ready to hit the stage.

I'm a little freaked out. I've seen the Metallica guys around but never really gotten near them or talked to them. Differing time schedules, contrasting socio-economic realities, and the fact that they are mega-huge rock stars and I'm the drum roadie for the opening band have conspired to keep our paths quite separate. Which is probably for the best, because I'm pretty much a drunken knucklehead and no good can come from interacting with these guys, all I can do is get myself, or worse yet the Suicidal guys, in trouble. But here it is.

"Um, what do you... what do you mean?" I stammer. Lars hoots with laughter. "What do I mean? Come on, man, didn't you just play a killer rock show out there?" I'm somewhat confounded, then with slowly dawning horror I realize he must think that I'M Jimmy, the drummer for Suicidal Tendencies. I guess we do look a little alike as far as both having long dark hair and Suicidal Tendencies t-shirts. And I'm sitting here in the ST dressing room eating a sandwich & drinking a beer after their show. I'm a few inches taller than Jimmy, but otherwise, it's a totally forgivable mistake.

By now the other Metallica guys are coming into the room to see what's happening. This keeps getting better and better. "Er, what rock show?" I sound like a complete dumbass but I have no idea what to do. Nothing in my experience has prepared me for something like this. I definitely don't want to embarrass the guy in front of his band. But he's making it really hard not to.

Lars is flabbergasted. He must think Jimmy is a really humble guy. "Come on, how was it out there tonight? You sounded great!" By now the whole band plus their stage manager are crammed into the room watching the exchange. I briefly think about bluffing and pretending to be Jimmy, but in a rare moment of good judgement I realize the only thing to do is be straight with the guy.

"Um, I think you have me confused with Jimmy. The drummer. In Suicidal Tendencies. I'm... um, I'm his roadie."

The room erupts in laughter as Lars blanches and mumbles something I don't quite hear. Mercifully the band leaves the room and heads for the stage.

I guess the Metallica roadies don't get to hang out in the dressing room. Sorry, dude. It was an easy mistake to make.

Towards the end of the 1994 Metallica/Suicidal Tendencies/Candlebox tour we started hearing rumors that Metallica was going to throw a huge "end-of-tour" party for everyone on the tour. For a 28-year-old roadie living his rock 'n' roll dream, this was fantastic news. The party was scheduled for the last day off of the tour, in Atlanta. Then we'd have a few more gigs to close out the tour before everyone headed home.

At this point the Suicidal roadies were pulling double-duty. Rob Halford, the legendary lead singer of Judas Priest had joined the tour with his new band, Fight. They didn't have a road crew, so we got drafted to help them out. It was pretty amazing to be working for Halford's band, and an extra paycheck? Hell yes. The only thing I liked better than being a roadie was getting paid to be a roadie. Twice. Fight's drummer was Scott Travis, who had played on the last couple of Priest albums. He was a super cool guy, very chilled out and a real pleasure to work with. He had this big purple double bass drum set with a metal cage holding everything up. I always felt like I was in a spaceship when I sat down to play his drum kit. They were only doing a handful of shows on the Metallica tour, and the whole Halford band was pretty much just happy to be there getting their new project out in front of these enormous Metallica audiences.

But it definitely made for some busy show days. First, we had to unload the Suicidal gear, get it set up and do our stage check. Then while Candlebox was setting up we'd unpack the Fight stage gear and get that set up. As soon as Candlebox was finished setting up we'd run the Fight gear out on stage in front of their stuff and do a fast line check before doors opened and the crowds started coming in. Fight would get out there and do their thing, then we'd tear down their stuff and load the truck while Candlebox was playing. Then as soon as we were finished loading out Fight's gear we had to do the Suicidal Tendencies show, and then load THEM out as fast as possible so Metallica could do their thing.

Everybody on the crew was ready for a big end-of-tour party when Atlanta rolled around. Metallica had rented out a big night club for the occasion. They had the party catered with amazing barbecue and southern cooking, and there was an open bar that we all were doing our best to drink dry. The party was packed with all the bands on the tour and their road crews. The Metallica guys weren't there yet, but the club had a separate room waiting for them. I was hanging out with Billy, our guitar tech, who went on to become a multi-platinum recording engineer for the supergroup Garbage, but back in 1994 we were just two roadies loading up on Metallica's free booze. Billy ended up marrying Shirley Manson, the incredibly talented and drop-dead gorgeous lead singer for Garbage. It's nice to see my old road buddy make good.

And load up we did. As the party started to wind down in the wee hours of the morning it was about time to find our way back to the hotel and try to get a few hours of sleep before load-in the next day. We had a show to do, and it was going to be a hot, humid rock show out in the blazing Atlanta sun. Staggering through the parking lot looking for a cab something even better suddenly appeared. A limo! Why should we pay for a taxi when there was a perfectly good stretch limo idling right there in the parking lot? I stumbled over to the big black vehicle and started knocking on the windows.

"Hey! HEY!" I shouted at the tinted windows. "Anybody in there? Gimme a ride, man!" The windows didn't reply. Fumbling with the door latches didn't have much effect, as the limo was locked tight against my unwelcome attempts at entry. If there was anyone inside they were doing a good job of ignoring me. As my plaintive entreaties for a free ride degenerated into incoherent boozy mumbling, Billy pulled me away and we set about finding another way to the hotel.

How did we get back to the hotel that night? I certainly don't recall. As a matter of fact, I don't recall much of anything for the rest of that evening until my alarm clock awoke me for bus call a few hours later. I dragged myself down to the tour bus with a horrific hangover that checked all the boxes... Headache? Yes. Nausea? You betcha. Mysterious aches and pains? Definitely. Embarrassment over my stupid behavior the night before? Not yet. That's one good thing about still being half-drunk in the morning, regret doesn't have a chance to set in yet. The plan is to simply try to survive the day.

And what a day it was! The Atlanta sun was shining, the birds were singing, and I felt like I was going to puke all over the drum set. Looking back, none of the roadies that day looked particularly bright-eyed or bushy-tailed. Everybody seemed to be sleepwalking through load-in and set up. Somehow we made it through soundcheck without any major mishaps. Heading for the Suicidal crew bus to try and take a short power nap before showtime, James from Metallica accosted me on the loading dock. "Hey man," he grinned down at me. "How you feeling?" I mumbled something about a headache, to which he responded, "Yeah, I saw you at the party last night. Trying to get into our car. You were lookin' pretty high." He strode off to be a mega-rock god and I shuffled off to be an embarrassed roadie taking a roadie nap on the roadie bus.

But, all hangovers eventually wear off, even the really bad ones, and soon we were ready to finish the summer trip across America with one last show in Miami. We did our usual double-duty with Fight and Suicidal then settled in to see Metallica kill it one last time. The show was insane, the Florida Metallica fans were going crazy, tearing up the muddy field and throwing these huge pieces of turf in the air and at each other. Rob Halford came out to sing the Judas Priest classic "Grinder" with Metallica and the place went absolutely nuts. Halford singing for Metallica was one of the coolest things I'd ever seen, and it reminded me how lucky I was to be out there seeing this amazing stuff happen right in front of my eyes. Talk about a rock 'n' roll dream come true.

After the Metallica tour ended Suicidal was heading over to Europe for another hit-and-run string of dates in Germany, Sweden, Belgium, France and England. We had this amazing rock 'n' roll band called the Wildhearts opening up. Those guys were cool as hell and just an amazing band, sort of a mix of the Beatles and AC/DC, with awesome songwriting and vocals but a street-wise rough edge. Our sound guy Tom liked them so much he started mixing sound for them on the tour, and I think he ended up doing some tours with them years later. It was a blast, we were there for a month and we only played about seven shows, so there was lots of time to get into trouble. Suicidal played what was probably their best show I ever saw at Le Zenith in Paris on this run. It was the second-to-last show of the tour and the band went all out. They asked all the roadies to wear ST jerseys and come out at the end of the show to sing backup vocals on the show closing song. The place was packed with over 6,000 Suicidal fans and they were going absolutely batshit crazy. It was amazing to be part of that kind of energy.

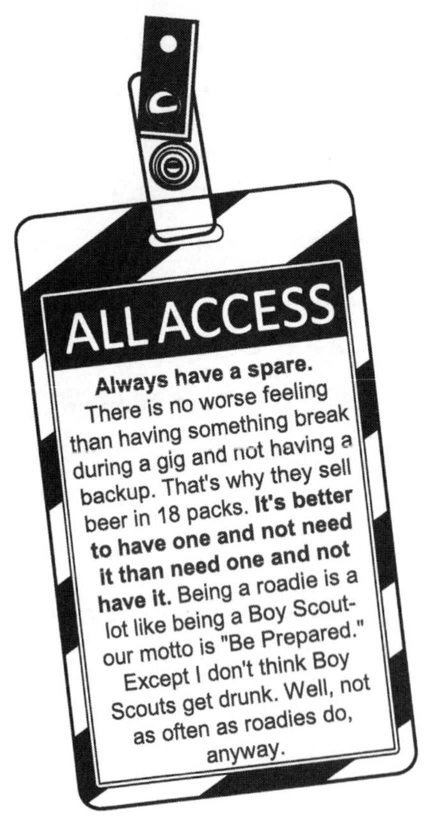

10 RACISM, SEXISM AND OTHER -ISMS

The touring industry was undergoing a profound change during my rock roadie career. The heavy metal dinosaurs that had once ruled the world were dead or dying, having been shoved unceremoniously into the tar pits of irrelevancy by Nirvana and Pearl Jam. Technology was growing at a lightning pace as something called the internet was being born. New ideas were replacing old ones everywhere you looked.

But one place that remain rooted in the past, at least as far as social awareness goes, was rock 'n' roll touring. Go figure, any business where it's a time-honored tradition to trade oral sex for backstage passes isn't going to be filled with the most forward-thinking folks. It was really backwards in many ways and looking back now, it seems crazy the stuff that was going on. Racism, prejudice and sexism were readily found in the white male-dominated business of rock touring. In the early 90's when I broke in, road crews were almost overwhelmingly made up of white men.

One of the bands on one tour I was on had a black man teching on their crew. I don't know if the racist stuff I was seeing and hearing was directed at him, or if it was just always there and I hadn't picked up on it before. But I definitely started to notice racist speech and actions on this particular tour. It didn't seem overt or in-your-face as far as I could tell, but there were racist jokes going around.

Changing a set list to incorporate cliched black phrases and expressions in lieu of the actual song titles, stupid shit like that. Now, let's be clear. I myself was not the most enlightened person during my touring career. I'm still not. So there is a good possibility this kind of abuse was much worse than I think and I simply wasn't picking up on it. Like I said, the people I worked on tour with were almost exclusively white dudes. And this was in the realm of hard rock/heavy metal. I'm not sure if other musical genres were more racially balanced, or more open and affirming. At the time there were still a lot of guys who had come up in the music business in the late 60's early 70's, so there was possibly some old, out of date thinking at work.

Ultimately there is no excuse for this attitude. I am sorry to say that I never stood up and called anybody out for this kind of bullshit, and that's just wrong.

Sexism was also an issue. When I first got out on some of these bigger tours I was shocked at how women were treated, and how some women at shows allowed themselves to be treated. Girls really did trade sex for backstage passes or tickets to concerts. Women really were sleeping with people on the tour, people were having sex in dressing rooms and tour buses, people were getting blow jobs backstage during drum solos. People were cheating on their lovers back home. And the attitudes towards women by some people on the tours was horrible. Girls at gigs were subject to being treated like sluts, verbally abused and completely disrespected.

Now, I was no angel. But abusing people was never my thing. I just didn't get that. I was definitely all for two grown people having a good time as long as everybody was enjoying. But it seemed like some of the guys on the road I encountered over the years really got into debasing women, like it was some kind of power trip. I tried to stick up for these girls when I could, but to my shame I never really went out on a limb or took a strong stance in this area.

LGBTQ issues? Not even on my radar at the time. I was clueless. I wasn't exactly what you'd call woke back in the day, so I can't speak to this at all. Looking back I'm sure it was pretty fucking tough to be on those tours and be anything other than a straight white man.

As far as the roadies go, there were very few women actually working on tours at that time. This is getting better now, but for the ten years I was out there, I only worked closely with one woman in a tech or production role. Carrie was the tour manager for Static X on the one tour I did with them, opening for Powerman 5000. She was an awesome tour manager. Also cool as hell. Towards the end of my time on tour women were making more inroads into the touring industry, especially on video production crews and other tech based job roles, so this situation is slowly changing for the better. It's about time. Even rock and roll has to change.

11 WE'RE NOT WORTHY

Nothing is sadder than a 28-year-old roadie sitting home, waiting for the phone to ring with a new tour offer. The road was now my true home, but Suicidal Tendencies was finished. As in broken up. Kaput. Over. This news broke my rock 'n' roll heart, because I loved Suicidal's music and wanted them to "make it", whatever that means. I imagine it would probably involve obscene amounts of cash, designer baseball caps and private planes for the roadies. Suicidal eventually reformed and started recording and touring again with Mike Muir singing and an all-new lineup. The new ST records are great and it's gratifying to see them still out there delivering the goods.

Sure, I sat in my darkened apartment back in Tucson surrounded by empty pizza boxes and dirty laundry playing video games and day drinking for a while. But eventually I had to figure out a way to make money. I started working whatever jobs I could get my hands on to make ends meet, including as a child care provider at a special-needs day care center. It actually made perfect sense, as my years of experience working with rock 'n' roll bands gave me a unique insight into the minds of disabled children.

Then there was that sweet gig as the house soundman at the historic Club Congress nightclub in downtown Tucson! Their regular house sound guy Fletch got hurt in a motorcycle accident, and once again who's there to make the save? I hadn't worked as a house sound guy in a long time, and it was a lot of fun getting to work at such a famous club. Being a "House Sound Guy" means that you do sound for any band booked at the venue who doesn't have their own sound engineer. In Tucson, where the bands are notoriously broke, that means almost all the bands. The plus side is that you might get to mix some awesome bands and you get to network your ass off, meeting tons of musicians and making some great contacts for future work. The downside is having to do sound for crappy cover bands. If I never have to mix some local cover band playing "Brown Eyed Girl" by Van Morrison, it'll be too soon. The most surreal soundman experience of all time happened during that stint at Club Congress at a Pork Torta gig. The Pork Torta are Tucson legends, a trio that play twisted rock complete with outlandish stage clothes. Getting the chance to mix sound for them enabled me to check off another box on my "Must-Rock" list. The only bad part was that they had a singing drummer. Singing drummers are the bane of any sound engineer's existence. Getting their vocals loud enough without screwing up the sound levels of the drum set is a real headache, and only the best sound guys out there can do it well. I was not one of those sound guys.

At Club Congress the house sound board used to be in this sort of alcove, frequently referred to as the "Audio Closet". You would make adjustments on the sound board, then pop out of the alcove into the room to listen, then pop back in to make adjustments. It was actually nice to have a private space if you wanted to take a break or get away from the insanity of a crowded club for a few minutes. We also mixed stage monitors from that same front-of-house sound board, as there was no dedicated monitor desk near the stage. So if the band needed any adjustments to the stage mix during the show they would have to ask for it over the PA.

The Pork Torta soundcheck went great, and everything was sounding good. The band seemed happy, and come show time the club is packed and it's looking like a good night. The band shows up at showtime in some sort of crazy 70's outfits. Cool! The Torta hits the stage and starts rocking. I'm popping back and forth to listen to the room, and then returning to the Audio Closet to make a few adjustments, and after a couple of songs it's dialed in and sounding tight.

I'm chilling out in the Audio Closet, checking audio meters and doing sound man stuff when all of a sudden the drummer starts bellyaching over the microphone. "Mister Soundman! I can't hear my vocals!" I turn up his vocal mic in his monitor a bit. After the next song ends he's at it again. "Mister Soundman! Please! I can't hear my vocals, can you turn it up?" Again I boost the vocal. It should be loud as hell now. But no, after the next song he's still up there, asking for more vocal. I step out of the Audio Closet to take a look at the stage. Maybe the drum monitor is unplugged or fell over or something. I make my way through the crowd to the edge of the stage and there's my answer. The drummer is wearing an old school Evel Knievel motorcycle helmet. With no ear holes. Of course you can't hear, you moron! I go back to the audio closet and turn his vocals OFF in his monitor. I didn't hear another peep out of him the rest of the night.

Finally, the phone rang. Salvation at last! Jimmy Degrasso was going on tour with Alice Cooper, and the gig sounded like it would be a good one, with a trip to South America. Jimmy had played with Alice previously. You probably saw him in the movie "Wayne's World". Jimmy is in Alice's band in the concert sequence, and he's also featured in that famous scene backstage where Wayne and Garth act like starstruck fanboys when they get to meet Alice. "We're not worthy! We're not worthy!"

ALL ACCESS
Protect your turf.
Real estate is invaluable on a rock 'n' roll stage. Make sure you have enough room for your stuff and room to work. Don't go crazy and hog up the whole place, but don't be Mister Nice Guy. You know what happens to Nice Guys? They finish last. And they end up having to tune their guitars in the men's room.

Alice Cooper was returning to touring after being off the road for five years. He was booked to play the Monsters Of Rock stadium concert series in South America, with shows in Sao Paulo, Rio, Santiago and Buenos Aires. Even factoring in the travel days and rehearsals it was only a few weeks of work, but when you're desperate to make your rock 'n' roll dreams come true, you take any grab at that brass ring you can get. Also, I couldn't handle another Pork Torta show.

Have you ever been to South America? It's a beautiful place, except for the parts that are fucking terrifying. Rehearsals for this tour were in Sao Paulo, Brazil. This was my first time in South America, and riding in the van from the airport seeing the way many of the people lived was utterly shocking for me. There were run down shacks lining the road from the airport all the way into the city. Families living in tiny huts made of cardboard boxes and wooden scraps, electrical cords hooked into street lights to steal electricity, people going through garbage cans looking for food. I had never seen real poverty like this before and it hit me hard. Miles and miles of this, all the way from the airport into Sao Paulo.

There was ample anxiety for me going into the Alice Cooper rehearsals, as this would be the first time I had gone out on a tour where I didn't know anybody on the crew. Yes, my first solo flight! Apron strings, begone! With Suicidal, the tour manager was my old friend Tom who I had known for years and worked with back in the clubs in Syracuse. But this would be a whole new environment for me, with an all-new cast of characters. Alice Cooper was also the biggest artist I had worked for yet, by far. I was nervous but excited and determined to do my best and make it work, or at least have fun trying. Nothing would be permitted to stand between me and the rock roadie life I dreamed of!

At rehearsals I met the rest of the touring crew. Ken Barr was one of the guitar techs, a big tattooed guy from NY with a great sense of humor. He would become one of my best friends on the road. Ken was actually my inspiration to write this book; his own tour autobiography "We Are the Road Crew" is a great look at touring life from his unique point of view. I highly recommend reading it. The other backline guy was Batty, an Irish guitar tech who had worked with Iron Maiden and a million other big acts. He was a wisecracking fun-loving sort of fellow. Those two had toured together many times with Alice. Ralph the lighting guy was lovable but the sort who is automatically the butt of every joke. It was just something in his DNA, maybe. Perhaps he was born with the "Kick Me" gene. He was all heart, though, and took the teasing in stride most of the time. The tour manager was Toby Mamis.

I was amazed to see the legendary Shep Gordon at the rehearsals. He's one of those guys I had read about but never expected to actually get to meet. Shep has been Alice's manager since 1968. Over the years he's managed a wildly diverse stable of entertainers including Groucho Marx! He single-handedly created the "celebrity chef" genre, guiding the careers of Wolfgang Puck and Emeril Lagasse, and is himself a tremendous cook. He was recently the subject of a documentary film directed by the famous actor Mike Myers, "Supermensch: The Legend Of Shep Gordon". Shep was super cool and always treated the crew and everyone on the tour great. After they finished up the "Alice Cooper Trashes

The World" tour back in the 90's Shep invited everyone on the tour - band, roadies, families - to his place in Maui where he put everyone up and fed them gourmet food he prepared himself.

Alice's band for this tour was Stef Burns on guitar, Paul Taylor on guitar and keyboards, Greg Smith on bass and Jimmy on drums.

The other roadies must have detected my trepidation, like sharks smelling blood or a cheetah spotting a gimpy antelope on the African plains. Batty and Ken tried to gang up on me with some good-natured hazing, but it didn't really work. I gave it right back to them, and we all eventually settled in on picking on Ralph the lighting guy. This tour gave me my first experience being in the Alice Cooper stage show. As anyone who's seen one of Alice's live concert extravaganzas can attest, there are loads of characters in the show besides Alice and the band - there's the doctor and his assistant who strongarm the Coop into a straightjacket during "The Ballad of Dwight Frye", the executioner who chops off his head with the guillotine, Cold Ethyl, Alice's living/dead girlfriend, the wife/punching bag from "Only Women Bleed", heck there's even a full street gang running around during "Gutter Cat vs The Jets"! Most of these roles are played by the roadies. Alice's wife and/or daughter come out on the road to play some of the parts that involve actual talent or choreography, but mostly it's us stage techs in the funny costumes up there beating the hell out of poor Alice.

South America was a blast. The shows were amazing, the Monsters of Rock shows are legendary, with hundreds of thousands of fans at the shows. Ozzy Osbourne, Megadeth and Faith No More all played too. The touring schedule was pretty laid back with a show every few days as the gear and staging was transported to the next city, so there was plenty of time to get into trouble. We spent most of our down time at the beach bars drinking at these little huts set up on the sand. It wasn't fancy but the beer was cheap and we had a great time busting Ralph's chops.

The Alice Cooper guys were real pros and I learned a few lessons from Ken. I had gotten into the bad habit of cracking a beer right after the last song of the set ended and having a couple of beers as we packed up and loaded the truck. Kenny put the kibosh on that nonsense right away. He was absolutely right. Loading those trucks is hard work and can be dangerous, especially if some dumbass is half-drunk in the back of a tractor-trailer full of heavy road cases stacked to the ceiling.

All too soon my first Alice Cooper tour was over and I was headed back to Arizona and more sound gigs at Club Congress. I could only hope I wouldn't be doing sound for any more singing drummers wearing motorcycle helmets.

The following summer I had just turned 30 when my old drummer buddy Jimmy Degrasso (who thankfully does NOT wear a motorcycle helmet while drumming) got ahold of me again. Alice Cooper was gearing up for a full summer tour in 1996, was I interested in another gig as his drum tech? Of course I was. My dream was to turn this into a year-round, full-time gig, not just a summer job. It was a real pain in the ass having to bail on whatever short term jobs I was able to find in Tucson and head back out on tour every time my phone rang. The Alice Cooper tour would start with two weeks of rehearsals in Cabo San Lucas, Mexico. We would be rehearsing right at Sammy Hagar's rock 'n' roll nightclub, the world-famous Cabo Wabo Cantina. Then we would kick off the tour with a live recording at Cabo Wabo and head out across America with the legendary German hard rock band, the Scorpions. Batty was back as guitar tech along with a new face, John Ciasulli. John was a cool guy who had worked on several previous Alice tours. The "family" vibe was always there with the Coop, evidenced by the fact that people kept coming back to work for him tour after tour.

Cabo San Lucas was a tropical paradise. White sand beaches, palm trees, and can you say tequila? Alice put us up at this beautiful resort hotel right down the street from the Cabo Wabo Cantina so we could walk to work every day. We'd start rehearsing at about 11 am and knock off around five. The club was huge, packed full of rock memorabilia, including these four immense bronze statues of the Van Halen guys. You know you've made it when you have people making immense bronze statues of you. It was also full of booze that we would start in on as soon as the work day was done.

Most days Sammy Hagar himself would be hanging around Cabo Wabo and setting us up with drinks and food after our rehearsals were finished for the day. The guy actually does make a tremendous margarita. He's a real "foodie", so the menu at Cabo Wabo was amazing, packed with top notch Mexican dishes, featuring fresh local ingredients. Sammy eventually wrote a book called "Are We Having Any Fun Yet?" It's half autobiography, half cookbook, and half rock 'n' roll philosophy. Okay, that doesn't add up quite right, but you get the idea. Math was never my strong suit. Sammy's a great guy and he made our stay at his club wonderful.

Cabo San Lucas has a bad rap as a cheesy tourist trap, but it made a great place to rehearse for a rock 'n' roll tour. American money went a long way, and literally nothing I was interested in buying cost more than a couple of bucks. A cold beer? Dollar. Tequila shot? Dollar. A plate of the best Baja fish tacos you've ever tasted? Two bucks. It was crazy, in a wonderful, crazy, drink-all-the-beer kind of way.

There was even a "gentlemen's club" for those so inclined. The "Mermaid's Strip Club" was across the street and a bunch of the band and crew guys would hang out there every night getting to know the locals up close and personal. It wasn't my scene, but I heard it got pretty wild in there.

Time flies when you're having fun and before I knew it we were doing the first show of the tour. Alice brought in a recording truck to tape the show for a live album. Since Alice is one of the most well-connected guys in the business he called in some favors to make sure the live album was extra-special. Rob Zombie, Slash and Sammy Hagar all performed with the Coop to add some extra star appeal to the live recording. Sammy played guitar and sang with Alice on the opening song of the concert, "School's Out". Sammy was a way better guitar player than I had thought he would be. I guess he was more known as a lead singer since he got into Van Halen, but the guy could really rip on guitar. I suppose it's easy to be overshadowed guitar-wise when you're in a band with Eddie Van Halen. Slash from Guns 'n' Roses played guitar on "Only Women Bleed" and "Lost In America". We didn't see much of him. He kind of showed up the night of the show and did his thing. His guitar tech Adam was there to take care of Slash's guitar needs. Even though he only played two songs Slash brought a ton of guitars with him so I guess he really did need a tech to handle it all. Rob Zombie sang on "Feed My Frankenstein", which is perfect for him since he's such a fan of the classic old Universal Studios Monsters like Wolfman, Dracula and Frankenstein. Turns out Rob is also a huge Alice Cooper fan, go figure.

It was hard to leave Mexico after having such a blast but the next day we were on a plane to El Paso, Texas to meet up with our tour bus and start the tour with the Scorpions. Alice was opening the show, which meant we were done working early every night. The Scorpions guys were really nice. Old, but nice. I guess that might sound funny coming from a guy who's out there roadie-ing for a guy who's pushing 70, but Alice really is one of those ageless people. Since he got off the booze and drugs and focused his addictive personality disorder on becoming the best golfer on earth he's really in great shape, all things considered. He's out there at Major League Baseball stadiums throwing out the first pitch, running around on stage like a guy half his age. Either the man has found the fountain of youth or the rumors about him selling his soul to the devil are true. Nah, he goes to church too much for that.

The Scorpions tour was a blast. Alice had a really solid band consisting of Reb Beach and Ryan Roxie on guitar, Paul Taylor on keyboards, Todd Jensen on bass and of course Jimmy on drums. Every day we loaded in around lunchtime, and did a quick sound check right before they opened the venue to the fans. We went onstage at 7pm or so and we were usually finished playing, with the truck all loaded and the first beer of the night opened, by 9pm. It was a nice break from loading in first thing in the morning and getting done around midnight every day. The band seemed to be having fun, and since we were opening the show Alice didn't have as many props and stage set pieces as usual, so it was more of a straight-ahead, stripped down rock 'n' roll show. My favorite part of the show was when the guitar player Reb would come skateboarding out on stage for the encore song, "School's Out". I kept waiting for him to eat it and break a wrist or something but luckily he managed to stay on the thing every night.

I got to travel to so many places as a roadie, places I'm sure I never would have had the opportunity to visit otherwise. Like Russia. Alice Cooper played there on one European tour I was working on, this must have been 1997 or so, when I was 31. It was really strange, the concert promoters hired translators to kind of guide us all around when we got there and make sure we didn't cause any international incidents. On our first day in Moscow we visited Red Square. It was so incredible to actually be in this place I had only seen in books. To see the Kremlin and St. Basil's Cathedral was pretty mind blowing. So much history.

I wanted to hang out at Red Square some more, so the rest of the guys got a ride back to the hotel from the concert promoter's people and I stayed behind. I figured I'd take a train or a cab or something back to the hotel later. I wanted to see some more sights and do some shopping. Who knew when I'd be back in Moscow, right? The promoter's people told me Moscow had a great train system that would get me back to the hotel easily. I had a subway map and the address of the hotel. How hard could it be? I had been finding my way around the world for years, so I said farewell to the gang and set out to explore on my own.

Moscow was huge and kind of intimidating. Everything seemed so old and strange. The buildings, the cars, the people, nothing was familiar. I loved it. The people I tried to talk to were friendly enough but English wasn't spoken in very many places other than shops or restaurants. I picked up some souvenirs, took a bunch of pictures, and then set out for the subway to head back to the hotel. I took this huge old escalator, with wooden scrollwork down to the train platform. It was so different from what I was used to in the US. Everything was handmade and old.

Once I got out my map I realized with slowly dawning dismay that finding my way was going to be harder than I had anticipated. All the signs in the city were in Cyrillic Russian letters. Normally in Europe I could at least sound out the street and train station names well enough to navigate. Here I couldn't even read anything! I started to get worried, it was getting late and I didn't see any cabs around. I consulted my map, searched the train schedule as best I could and took my best guess at which train to get on.

It turned out to be the wrong train. At the next station I had to start all over again. I asked for help from a shop keeper at the station but he didn't understand me very well. By trial and error (make that lots and lots of errors) I painstakingly made my way slowly back towards the hotel. Eventually it became a matter of pride. By God, I didn't need any God Damned Russian taxicab to get home! I was going to find my own way back. On my own!

Finally I started to recognize some shops and buildings. I was getting close! I kept walking. By now I had been trying to find my way back for several hours, and I was hungry and exhausted. Then I saw a sign for the hotel! I was almost there! Victory was mine as I stumbled into the lobby and headed up to my room. I swore off exploration for a while after that one.

Everything in Russia was difficult. The airport was a complete nightmare. There didn't appear to be any lines, just crowds of people milling around. The promoter's crew seemed to have only the faintest idea of what they were supposed to do to get us into the country. I found myself wondering if they had done this before. That seemed to be a common thread - the people in all the Eastern Bloc countries were nice enough and meant well, and they tried really hard, but ultimately they didn't seem very good at their jobs. They got an "A for Effort" most of the time, but never really delivered the goods like you needed them to.

The Eastern Bloc concerts were crazy. Like the time Alice played an outdoor festival stage for a huge crowd in Budapest. The local sound system and stage equipment was old and malfunctioning, as was the local stage crew. Our guys did their best to cobble it together so we could do the show. Our monitor guy, Tater, was in a special kind of Roadie Hell reserved only for monitor engineers. The monitor engineer is the guy responsible for making sure Alice can hear himself sing on stage, and this sound system was barely hanging on at line check. Once Alice arrived the band hit the stage and the show started. At one point the monitor board completely stopped working, so the band couldn't hear themselves onstage. They kept playing as Tater scrambled to sort out the problem. I saw the local sound guys come running up on stage with another sound board from the truck. They literally threw it on top of the broken one and started plugging it in. It was amazing. Tater was trying to mix sound for Alice Cooper on a pile of broken Russian sound boards... and somehow got it all working again. He was just like Scotty on Star Trek.

After the show the urban myth that Russia has the best Vodka in the world was robustly tested. Good news, comrades! They do.

12 ALICE COOPER IS ACTUALLY A REALLY, REALLY NICE GUY

Imagine a stadium full of rioting European biker gangs. Well, that's where I used to work, so don't ever complain about your office cubicle again. Alice Cooper was playing a big Biker Festival somewhere in Europe. At these bigger gigs, the local promoter provides labor to help the touring crew with the concert - unloading trucks, moving road cases, loading the trucks at the end of the night, stuff like that. These folks are called stage hands, and for this gig, the local stage hands were all bikers, members in good standing of the local organizations. Load in went without incident, as the European bikers were strapping lads well-suited for the task at hand. The show went well, with an enthusiastic crowd of motorcycling enthusiasts drinking heavily, beating each other up, urinating everywhere and cheering on the Coop's antics with gusto. Things got out of hand and the local authorities dispersed the rowdier elements. Just another night in my world on tour. Rock 'n' roll shows in Europe are a lot like the football (or soccer for us Americans) games that occasionally erupt in some sort of fisticuffs and mayhem. Just another one of the many fun fringe benefits of international travel!

At the end of the night we started breaking down the gear and loading the trucks. But the stagehands were nowhere to be found. Turns out our local helpers had been among those dispersed earlier. They must have enjoyed the fun so much they decided to call it a night when the concert ended and go home. Or off to a bar to keep the party going. In any case, they weren't there to help us load out.

The stage full of equipment loomed large. It wasn't going to load itself into those trucks. We resigned ourselves to completing the night on our own. Normally the backline crew - the roadies who deal with the band's stage gear like guitars, amps and drums - would be finished packing up the stage gear and loading out in about 30 minutes. Tonight however we stayed to help with ALL the gear...sound, lighting staging, all of it. EVERYONE stayed to help until the whole production was packed up and loaded onto the trucks. This took considerably longer than usual, since where normally we would have 30-40 people on the load out crew tonight we had only a handful of people to do it all. It was also a fuck of a lot more work. The old show biz saying "The Show Must Go On...And The Truck Must Be Loaded" holds true. We had to get finished and hit the road as soon as possible in order to make it to the next show on time. Everybody on the whole crew was all in that night.

It was an exhausted and extra-grumpy group of roadies that loaded in at the next show the following morning. As we waited for the band to show up for sound-check, Alice's manager Toby showed up a bit early. "Alice heard about what happened last night. He says thanks." With that Toby handed each of us a crisp $100 dollar bill.

We went from grumpy to grateful pretty quickly. Alice didn't have to do that. Being a roadie is a great gig but sometimes it sucks, and the possibility of having to load all the trucks by yourself if the local bikers/stagehands get wasted and bail on you is part of what you sign on for when you take the gig. But Alice is old school. Make that Old School. He came up in a different time and so he does things a little differently. The guy has been on the Muppet Show AND Hollywood Squares, for cryin' out loud. Not at the same time however. Even Alice Cooper couldn't do that.

ALL ACCESS
When the record company people offer to buy a round for the tour personnel at an after party don't be an asshole and order three drinks at once. I used to do this all the time when I was a young idiot/alcoholic. **Be cool when somebody is being cool to you.** You can always order another round on their tab when nobody's looking.

Every crew feels a bit like a family on a long tour, but with Alice it was even stronger. The vibe on all the Alice Cooper tours I did was different from anything I experienced before or since. Not sure if it was because Alice and his management had been together for so long, or because so many people on the crew had been around for many Alice tours. Maybe it was because the Coop's actual family was around so much. But working for Alice really did feel like being part of a family. Alice went the extra mile for us many times when he didn't have to. On days off Alice would frequently get invited to throw out the first pitch at pro baseball games. He's a baseball nut so he did this as often as the schedule allowed. He would always invite the band & crew to come along and hang out in the VIP Suite at the stadium to watch the game. We were all being paid damn well for our work. The extra stuff wasn't required, But Alice Cooper is just that kind of guy. Like when we were in Switzerland, he got all us roadies Swiss Army knives with our names engraved on them.

At the end of one tour I was flying home from the last show. At the airport I was headed to the departure lounge at my gate for the flight to Phoenix, where I'd connect to my flight home to Tucson. There was Alice, who lives in Phoenix. He saw me. Now, Alice is always super cool. But there's a difference between interacting onstage, at a production rehearsal or in a group, and hanging out in the airport together waiting for a flight. But, the Coop had seen me and was waving me over to have a seat.

“Hey boss,” I said.

“J Mann, hi. Whatcha reading?” Alice gestured at the book I had clutched in my hand to read on the flight. He's always so cool and friendly.

I looked down at the book in my hand. I had actually forgotten I was holding it in my current state of anxiety over having to log face time with a Rock Legend. I read the title and grimaced.

"Uh, it's a collection of erotica...short stories...about vampires," I stammered sheepishly.

Alice smiled up at me beatifically and shrugged. "I usually just read the Bible."

I looked down. Alice was, indeed, reading a Bible.

FUELING UP ON TOUR
IN MONTREAL DRUMMING
FOR UNCLE SAM-1989
MY FAMOUS BILL WARD
IMPRESSION - JUNE '83
HATE
FUELING THE HATE
IN TURIN, ITALY
ON THE ROAD OPENING
FOR METALLICA-1993
MASTERS OF REALITY!
MY VERY FIRST
TOUR BUS!-1990
DRUMMING FOR
UNCLE SAM-1989

MEGADETH
TOUR WITH
AC/DC
2001
ME (AND AN UNIDENTIFIED
SPECIAL FRIEND) AT THE
LOST HORIZON
1991
SYRACUSE, NY
A DRUM ROADIE'S VIEW OF
SUICIDAL TENDENCIES
OPENING FOR
METALLICA
1993

13 THE AMERICAN DREAM IS ALIVE AND WELL

I stand before you as living proof that the American dream is indeed alive and well. In school, we're all told the same old story, that America was founded as a nation where if you worked hard and followed your dreams anything was possible. I know, I know, it sounds like bullshit, but all I know is this: it worked for me. When I fell in love with rock 'n' roll music and unwittingly chose to dedicate my life to being a part of it, I started on a path that took me to places and gave me experiences I never imagined possible. Well, possible for me. My folks split up when I was a little kid, and growing up in the ice and snow of rural upstate New York, dreams were in short supply. My friends all seemed to have such lame goals. They longed to own a cool dirt bike, or a fishing boat. A keg party on the weekend. A job that was bearable enough to keep going back to year after year to pay the bills and make ends meet. I didn't have the slightest idea what I wanted to be when I "grew up", but the one thing I did know was that there was absolutely nothing happening in my hometown that inspired me in the slightest.

Until I discovered rock music. I was utterly directionless up to the moment that rock 'n' roll captured my imagination and gave me something to dream about, something to live for. It gave me a goal. It gave me a dream. It gave me a family. I didn't choose rock 'n' roll. Rock 'n' roll chose me. It was all

I wanted. I busted my ass working tirelessly to make it in the music business, and the best part is, I didn't even realize I was working at it! I was just out there having fun. Only later, looking back, did I realize that I was diligently chasing my dream and kicking ass non-stop 24 hours a day to make that dream a reality.

And it happened. My dream came true. I traveled the world with rock bands. I played in cool bands. I hung out with Lemmy from Motorhead. I made it with girls with big hair and spandex pants (Yes, the 80's were awesome). Sure, the first gigs I did kind of sucked. Sure, I worked with tons of shitty bands, and rode in the back of unheated moving vans to load PA stacks into filthy dive bars. I never dreamed at the time that it was all moving me towards my ultimate destiny, traveling the world and making a living doing what I loved. I am so grateful that my dream really did come true.

14 CLOWN SUITS AND SNAKE POOP

One of the best parts about being a roadie for Alice Cooper was actually getting to be part of the stage show. Alice is famous for his elaborate stage presentations, where he is attacked, imprisoned in a straitjacket, and executed in some particularly unsavory ways, including hanging, beheading and electrocution. What I didn't know when I started working for the Coop was that the cast of characters that appears in the Alice Cooper stage show are actually the roadies and crew members in costume. Alice's wife and daughter, both trained actresses and dancers, appear in the show too, but mainly it's us roadies. I'm a bit of a ham and the idea of being onstage with Alice sounded great to me, despite the understandable stage fright that goes hand in hand with being on stage with a Rock 'n' Roll Hall Of Fame alumni.

My debut role in the Alice Cooper show was a thug in the street gang that takes on Alice and the band during the song "Gutter Cat vs The Jets". The other roadies and I would dress up like some sort of cliched 50's street gang back behind the amps and then run out on stage to fight with Alice. Naturally we got our asses kicked every time, to the delight of the audience. When we played in Tucson a bunch of my friends came to the show. During "Gutter Cat" they made their way to the front and started throwing things up on stage. I was too busy "acting" to take much notice of exactly what they were flinging at me. After the show was over we discovered they had been tossing XXL granny panties on stage with endearing love notes to me written on them in magic marker. Things like "I love you J Mann," and "Meet me after the show, sonny". Those guys!

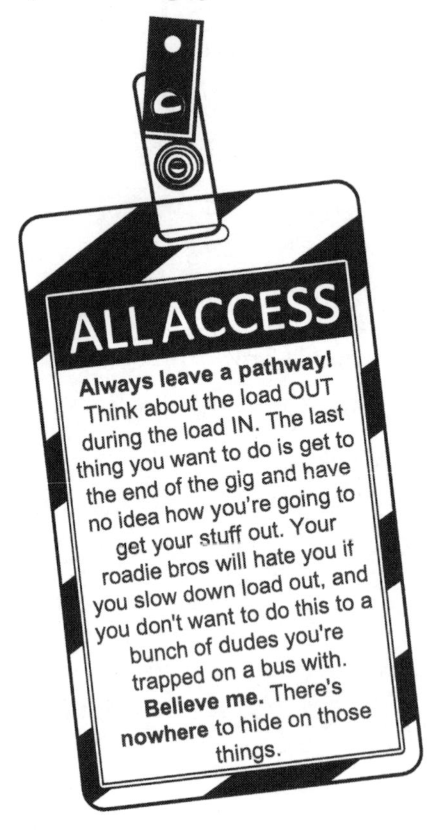

ALL ACCESS
Always leave a pathway! Think about the load OUT during the load IN. The last thing you want to do is get to the end of the gig and have no idea how you're going to get your stuff out. Your roadie bros will hate you if you slow down load out, and you don't want to do this to a bunch of dudes you're trapped on a bus with. **Believe me.** There's **nowhere** to hide on those things.

Next I was an evil clown from the Alice Cooper Rock 'n' Roll Carnival. For the uninitiated, evil clowns look just like regular clowns, with the big primary-colored pom pom covered polyester outfits and oversized shoes, but we had demonic clown masks and wigs to top it all off. Also knives. The evil clowns would attack Alice throughout the show, and finally seal him in an iron maiden - not the band, the medieval torture device - and stab him with swords. Somehow he cheated death every time and came back to life to finish the concert. Thank goodness, since he was the guy signing the paychecks.

How the hell are you supposed to go out on stage in front of 70,000 screaming Alice Cooper fanatics in Finland or wherever and stab their hero in the neck with a sword? Sure, it's a fake sword, and he knows you're going to do it (hell, he's paying you to do it) but still. Talk about stage fright! Even after years of being onstage as a drummer and stage tech, at those huge festivals in front of all those people it was nerve wracking. Really we were just out there goofing around in silly clothes and having fun. What got me through having to go from roadie to rock 'n' roll stage actor? Alice was just so cool to work for, and the vibe on all his tours was really laid back and low pressure. That helped a lot. He had a crew of true professionals, besides me, and we always got the job done for him, even in the weirdest circumstances.

For the "Brutal Planet" tour the roadies became paramilitary prison guards from a dystopian future. Pat the production manager even played the part of a mutant cyborg who introduced the band after we wheeled him out on stage in his enormous robot outfit at the beginning of the show. We really got into character on that tour, and instead of only suiting up for the shows we started wearing our military gear all day long. Which got us some strange looks at the mall. If we tried that now we'd probably end up on some sort of terror watch list.

Then there was the time Alice Cooper hit me in the face with a pie. I know, right? The guy is so old school. Nobody else would think of that! It was at my last show on the 1999 tour, as I was leaving Alice's tour early to start up on another tour with a different band. Alice was cool about it, and we had found a substitute drum tech to come out and cover me for the shows I would miss. My last gig with Alice was coincidentally in Syracuse, New York, my home town, which made it even weirder. At the end of the concert all the characters in the show are supposed to come out on stage as the band finishes the final song and wave at the crowd as the show ends. As I was out there in my clown suit and mask, waving at the audience as planned, suddenly my mask got yanked off my head. I looked around in shock and that's when Alice Cooper hit me in the face with a big gooey banana cream pie. I guess it was his way of saying goodbye and thanks for all the hard work. He had a big smile on his face as he did it, too. After torturing and killing him onstage all year I guess I had it coming.

At Alice Cooper shows the sickest moments aren't planned - they just seem to happen. Alice is famous for bringing out a boa constrictor and wearing it around his neck during his concerts. Most of the snakes are loaned to Alice by his legions of devoted fans around the world. Bringing a large snake on tour and providing the very specialized care a reptile like that requires is a major undertaking, so it's easier to just have the snake delivered each night. Alice's personal assistant had a rolodex of snake-owning Alice Cooper fans around the globe and would just coordinate the snakes in advance. We got our snake to use for the night, the reptile-loving Alice Cooper fan gets in for free and gets to meet Alice. It's a win-win for everyone.

I don't know how often large boa constrictors take a shit. I assume it's infrequent. They only eat once a month or something, so how often do they need to relieve themselves, really? During a show in Los Angeles Alice was out there, doing his thing, with the snake around his neck. Suddenly the snake starts shitting. I mean really shitting. I'm not sure what this thing had eaten, but whatever it was, it was big. Big, and indigestible. Now Alice has snake poo all over his leather pants, and there's a sizable mound of snake poo on the stage. One of our sharp-eyed roadies spots the crisis and dashes out there with a towel to save the day. Not me. I was watching from way back by the drum set. It seemed safer.

Now, boa constrictors eat meat, so snake poop is basically composed of rotten meat. And if there's one thing that rotten meat is good at, it's smelling horrible. Our guy kneels down on the stage in front of Alice and the snake and starts trying to towel up the snake poo. The towel kind of breaks open the snake poo pellets and releases it's horrible stench. Our guy gets a whiff of the snake poop stench and starts vomiting. Now he's trying to wipe up the snake poo and his own puke. Another roadie runs out to help. He smells the combination of snake shit and roadie vomit and, you guessed it, he starts puking too. Hilarity ensues.

Alice Cooper, ever the consummate professional, just keeps singing.

15 MEET THE NEW BOSS, SAME AS THE OLD BOSS (EXCEPT WITH DIFFERENT DRUM STICKS)

Rock 'n' roll is a fast-paced business and if you're going to make it as a touring rock roadie you have to stay flexible. I'm not talking about yoga, although I did get deeply into that stuff years after I retired from touring. Things change fast and all good roadies have to be able to roll with the punches and adapt on the fly. Like in 1998, I was 32 and in my natural habitat, out on tour with Alice Cooper, working for drummer Jimmy Degrasso. Things were going great until Jimmy got a call from Megadeth. Their drummer Nick Menza was having health problems and they needed a new drummer fast. Megadeth were out on tour with Ozzfest and there was no way they were going to cancel those shows. Jimmy knew the Megadeth guys from when Suicidal Tendencies opened up for them back in 1992 (remember when the drum riser almost collapsed at my very first Suicidal Tendencies show in Miami because I was a dumbass newbie?) and he had played on a Dave Mustaine solo project called MD45. Dave Mustaine is the lead singer, lead guitarist, and founder of Megadeth. More on him later.

This was a big opportunity for Jimmy, so he went for it. Megadeth already had a good drum tech who was also their production manager, so I wouldn't be going along. I thought that meant I was going to be out of a job. Instead, I stayed on with the Alice Cooper tour to be the drum tech for Jimmy's replacement. Confused yet? Wait, it gets weirder. The new drummer was Eric Singer. Eric had played with Alice prior to his first stint drumming for KISS. He made history as the first blonde in KISS. Eric had left KISS when the band decided to reunite their original lineup for the first of many "farewell tours", so he was available and ready to go when Alice called on him. I guess it really is a small rock 'n' roll world.

Eric is a great guy and working for him was a blast. He is an avid collector of expensive watches, bordering on an obsession. He even gave me a beautiful Swiss watch as a gift after one Alice Cooper tour we did together.

My favorite part about working for him over the years was watching his onstage showmanship. Eric is great at making playing the drums in a rock 'n' roll band look like the coolest thing anyone could possibly do - which it pretty much is. He's an expert at what we call "stick tricks", like twirling his drum sticks, flipping his drum sticks, and throwing his drum sticks in the air and catching them again, all without missing a beat. After doing so many shows with Eric I got to know his routine pretty well, and one of his favorite stick tricks was to end a song with a big beat on the snare drum and then toss a stick high overhead and catch it as it came down. The problem was, at the end of the song the lighting guy normally blacks out the stage, so Eric would usually fumble the catch in the darkness. One night I got the bright idea to train my flashlight on the stick as it came down so Eric could see it. The first time I tried it he made the catch, looked at me in surprise and gave me a big smile. It wasn't rocket science, but on a long rock 'n' roll tour, you find silly little ways to pass the time and keep yourself amused. Kind of like in jail. From then on I kept going for it, and we did pretty well at it. Maybe that's why he got me that cool watch.

16 DEAD BABIES, DEAD BODIES, AND HOW TO GET YOURSELF KILLED ON TOUR

Ever seen a dead body? Not at a funeral, I mean just a dead body on the side of the road. I had this fun experience while I was on tour with Alice Cooper. That makes total sense, right? Where else would you be more likely to stumble across a random corpse? One time Alice had a gig in Montreal, Quebec and my buddy Tater and I were exploring the neighborhood near the hotel. Turns out we were in a pretty bad part of town, or as bad as any part of town in Canada gets. While narrowly avoiding being mugged we actually happened across a rock 'n' roll club I had played at back in the 80's when I was the drummer in Uncle Sam, the Rochester, NY based hard rock outfit that toured the East Coast in a graffiti-covered renovated school bus. I detailed those adventures elsewhere in this book. The club was called "Les Foufounes Electriques", which translates into English as "The Electric Buttocks". Best name ever! It's still around today, maintaining its status as Montreal's divey-est dive bar. They attract a lot of internationally touring bands as one of the coolest underground places to play in Canada. I was freaking out when Uncle Sam played there because the bass player from proto-thrash metal legends Voi Vod came to see us play. Well, actually he pretty much hung out there all the time when Voi Vod wasn't on tour because the club let him drink for free, but still, he was there when my band played!

As we headed back to the hotel we saw an ambulance and a police car pulled up on the sidewalk. Then we saw the dead guy they were there to pick up. Turns out that area was a notorious shooting gallery and the guy had probably OD'd the night before and spent the night on the sidewalk.

The closest I've come to actually becoming a dead body also happened on tour with Alice Cooper. We were doing a show in Ohio at an outdoor venue called the Nautica Stage in 1997. It's a wonderful outdoor concert venue right next to where the Cuyahoga River meets Lake Erie, just down the expressway from the Rock 'n' Roll Hall Of Fame. The day started out overcast and as we got closer to showtime the weather worsened dramatically. Right before Alice was scheduled to take the stage it was pouring rain and gale force winds were blowing in off Lake Erie. To make matters worse, lightning was striking all around the stage - with all the metal lighting trusses and sound towers on deck we were basically one big lightning rod. However, Alice was determined to do the show. Putter, our production manager, was able to convince him to cut the show a bit short, but they played. I spent the whole time crouched down behind the drum riser praying I wouldn't be electrocuted by a lightning strike or crushed to death when the stage collapsed. Apparently Alice is on good terms with Jesus or Buddha or Allah or whoever decides these things and they finished the show with no disasters, natural or otherwise. Somehow we escaped Cleveland with no casualties. Which is more than I can say for their pro football team.

Then there was the time I fell off the stage in Vienna, Austria while on tour with Megadeth. One of my duties on that tour was to measure the stage when we first arrived at the venue so we could figure out how much rock 'n' roll we could fit on it. When the band designed the stage show for that tour they had been planning to play arenas and large theatres. Over the course of the tour, however, reality began to set in and the venues started getting smaller and smaller as the tour wore on. We went from playing arenas to theatres to halls to big rock clubs to small nightclubs. So the stage that was designed for a 25,000 seat hockey rink was kind of hard to squeeze onto the stage of a club that holds 750 people. So I measured the available stage size and the production manager did the required math to figure out how many Marshall stacks we could fit on it.

On this beautiful morning in Vienna I stumbled out of the tour bus with my tape measure in hand to measure the stage. The venue had a modular platform stage, made up of 4 x 4 stage deck sections on legs, that lock together. I started my measuring work, hooking the end of the tape on the edge of the stage and backing up, paying out the tape as I went. Suddenly I backed right off the end of the stage. The stage crew had left out two sections of staging for the monitor desk to fit into, which I hadn't seen in the darkened hall. I fell five feet to the concrete floor. I came down hard, mostly on my ass, but cracking my head on the cement hard enough to see stars. After gathering my wits I limped to the Production Office seeking sympathy or First Aid. Sadly, both were in short supply. I put some ice on my head where a big knot was rising, and took a few aspirin, then went back to work. I was in pretty bad shape for a few days until the tour manager was finally able to get a German doctor to come see me. German doctors are supposed to be great, but mine spoke zero English and my High School German classes were long forgotten. Despite the communication barrier we managed to get the basics across. Head hurt. Need drugs. What's the German word for muscle relaxer? He gave me some kind of injection that seemed to help with the pain and I was feeling well enough to roadie at my usual superhuman level a few days later.

Another brush with death happened in 1994 while on tour in Europe with Suicidal Tendencies when I was just 27. One of the coolest things about touring in Europe are the ferry boats. In order to get to Scandinavia from mainland Europe you usually take a ferry boat. The boats are huge, the tour buses drive right into parking garages on the lower decks and park there during the trip. Once you're on board the party starts! Bars? Take your pick, there are plenty to choose from. Restaurants? You bet, have you tried the "All-You-Can-Eat" Lutefisk Buffet? Casinos? Damn right! Discos, night clubs, cigar bars, and shopping malls, the ways to entertain yourself on one of these fun boats are endless. If you're a V.I.P. or other high-ranking rock star you might even get one of their luxury suites. These ferries are basically short cruise trips, and are always lot of fun and a great break from the stress of the tour for us roadies. The trip takes about 17 hours one way and it's a hell of a way to spend a day off.

We traveled from Sweden back to mainland Europe on the MS Estonia after a show in Stockholm. When we got to Amsterdam we heard the horrible news: the Estonia sank in the middle of the night on her way back to Sweden. Apparently the doors on the bow of the ship failed and the ship began taking on water en route to Stockholm. Of the 989 people on board 852 died or were lost at sea. Rescue crews estimate over 700 people were trapped inside as the ship went down, and are still there to this day, as recovery efforts in that region are nearly impossible. Most died from drowning or hypothermia, the water temperature in the Baltic Sea was about 50 degrees that night. It ranks as one of the worst maritime disasters of the 20th Century. After the Titanic it is the second-worst European shipwreck disaster to have occurred in peacetime. We heard about it as we were setting up for a show in Amsterdam and just couldn't believe it. I was pretty freaked out. Can you imagine what that must have been like to wake

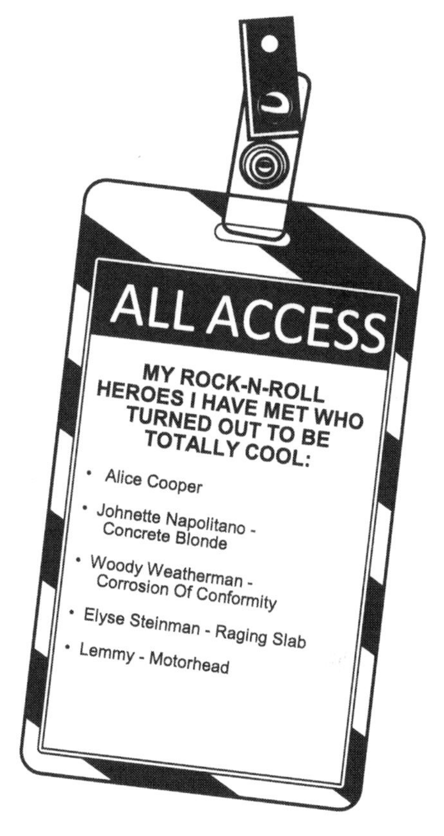
ALL ACCESS
MY ROCK-N-ROLL HEROES I HAVE MET WHO TURNED OUT TO BE TOTALLY COOL:
• Alice Cooper
• Johnette Napolitano - Concrete Blonde
• Woody Weatherman - Corrosion Of Conformity
• Elyse Steinman - Raging Slab
• Lemmy - Motorhead

up down in the depths of that huge ship as it went down, and being unable to get out as it filled up with ice cold water? We took another ferry trip to England a few days later and I stayed up top the whole trip. I just couldn't go down into the ship. Too many ghosts down there.

17 HELLO, NEW MILLENNIUM

Remember the Y2K panic? At the stroke of midnight on December 31, 1999, all our computers and electronic devices were going to stop working, the world would be plunged back into the Stone Age, industry would come crashing to a halt, and humanity would have to start over again. Total chaos! We'd all be living in caves and mating on animal skins to propagate the species. Actually, that last part sounds sort of good to me. Alice Cooper performed a special New Year's Eve concert at his Phoenix sports bar (appropriately named "Alice Cooper'stown") in 1999 to welcome the New Millennium. He called it the Millennium Masquerade Ball. I happened to be in Phoenix at the end of December, so I stuck around a few days to hang out with the gang and ring in the new year with Alice and the gang.

If there's one thing everyone likes to do around the holidays it's get together with old friends. I called my old buddy Tater, Alice's monitor engineer, when I got to town and found out where Alice was rehearsing. I headed over to say hello to Tater and see what was up. The band was working on a song, but when Alice spotted me, he stopped in the middle of the song and came over to give me a hug. It was weird, embarrassing and awesome all at the same time. Tater shouted, "J. Mann! You've officially become a rock celebrity!"

It was great to see everybody. I said it before, working for Alice Cooper always felt like a family.

Hanging out at rehearsal I managed to weasel my way onto the crew for the New Year's Eve show doing lights. The show was a blast, we drank plenty of champagne at midnight, and sadly, the much-talked-about Y2K "bug" never materialized. So much for mating on animal skin rugs.

The show was intended to be a formal masquerade affair, or what passes for a formal affair for Alice Cooper fans. Only 300 tickets were made available to the public, at $500 each. They included dinner at Cooper'stown and a private concert with Alice Cooper and the band. The crowd was made up of only the most hardcore, die-hard Alice Cooper fans. One of the coolest things about working for Alice has always been his fans. They are a diverse group. Or is it perverse? Anyway, you get all types at an Alice Cooper concert...goths, rockers, metalheads, punks, old, young, male, female, you name it. They are all delightfully weird in their own way and totally dedicated. We would see them patiently waiting outside shows around the world to try to meet Alice, with bags of stuff for him to autograph. In the rain, in the snow, in the blistering heat, Alice's creepy army of fanatical followers would be there waiting.

Of course, like the saying goes, "It's not what you know, it's who you know". The best way to get into any Cooper concert to meet Alice was always through his personal assistant, Renfield. His real name was Brian Nelson, but he was always known better by the name of Count Dracula's dedicated and insane insect-eating devotee. Brian got his job working for Alice mostly because he was the most dedicated Alice Cooper fanatic out there.

Born in Buffalo, New York, Brian started going to Alice Cooper concerts in 1973. His first show was on New Year's Eve on Alice's legendary "Billion Dollar Babies" tour, considered by many to be the most excessive, over-the-top rock spectacle ever produced. Brian was hooked, and threw himself wholeheartedly into following Alice around the world. Renfield had garnered an amazing collection of Alice Cooper memorabilia over the years, including a pair of leopard skin boots from Alice's "Billion Dollar Babies" Tour, a gold jacket Alice wore from back in the Spiders days, and this crazy leather bondage outfit the Coop once wore on tour. Frighteningly, legend has it he even got ahold of Alice's birth certificate, old passports, and recording contracts. The Rock And Roll Hall Of Fame Alice Cooper display was mostly taken from Brian's collection. Brian even had custom business cards made up proclaiming him the "World's Biggest Alice Cooper Fan". Following the "Flush The Fashion" tour Renfield heard Alice was in the market for a personal assistant and somehow got the Coop on the phone to ask for the job. Alice probably figured he'd be better off having this wacko working for him where he could keep an eye on him than letting him run around loose buying up his personal documents.

Brian was a weird guy, go figure, but was always super cool to me. He acted in the stage show with us on tours, usually playing the doctor who gets strangled by Alice when the Coop breaks free from the straight jacket during "The Ballad Of Dwight Frye". Brian's legs were even featured on the back cover of Alice's "Constrictor" album. Brian and I went to go see "The Blair Witch Project" in Fresno on a day off from a Cooper tour. Brian loved horror movies, and completely freaked out when these teenagers a few rows in front of us started making noise during the movie. Renfield stood up and started screaming at them until the manager came and made the kids leave. I think the manager was too afraid of Brian to kick us out too.

Brian Nelson passed away in 2009. This is the official press announcement Alice released upon learning of his death:

June 14th 2009

"It is with extreme sadness that we need to inform the community of Alice Cooper fans of the passing of Brian "Renfield" Nelson, Alice's long-time archivist and personal assistant. It was a sudden, completely unexpected, and untimely passing. We would appreciate it if you would keep him in your thoughts, appreciate his many contributions to Alice's life and career over the years, and respect Brian's privacy and the privacy of Alice and his extended family (at home and on tour) at this time."

Thanks for everything Brian, I hope you find peace wherever you are.

18 ROADIE-ING IS MY BUSINESS (AND BUSINESS IS GOOD)

The life of a rock 'n' roller is full of twists and turns, and staying open-minded is one of the most important skills you can have. You never know where you're going to wake up, or who you're going to end up working for. Jimmy Degrasso got ahold of me while I was in the middle of the Alice Cooper US/Canada tour in 1999. I was 32. Jimmy had left Alice's band the year before to join up with Megadeth, which was a great gig and a big break for him. Megadeth was a major act with their most recent album selling over a million copies, certified Platinum. He was finally a full member of a band again instead of being a hired gun or side - man. Megadeth needed a drum tech for their upcoming tour supporting their new album "Risk" starting in October. I was scheduled to tour with Alice until his tour ended around Halloween, but Megadeth was starting their tour on October 8. Megadeth had dates scheduled for the rest of the year, and into 2000, and I really wanted the gig. That was a lot of money to pass up. I spoke with Alice's management and they were cool with me splitting before the end of the tour, but only if I could find a replacement drum tech to finish the tour for me.

After many phone calls - remember this was before email was a thing - we tracked down Charlie Milton, a NY based roadie who was happy to get a couple of weeks of work filling in for me. Eric was bummed out I was splitting, but he is one guy who understands that in show business, business is business. After my farewell pie-in-the-face performance with Alice in Syracuse, which I describe in some detail elsewhere in this book, it was off to Phoenix to join up with Megadeth.

My first gig with the band was at the Arizona State Fair. I arrived on show day. Luckily, Gary, the band's production manager, had been the drum tech for Jimmy during the previous Megadeth tour opening for Iron Maiden in Europe, so he was able to show me how the kit worked and help get things going. Gary, or "Gaz" as everyone called him, was from Buffalo, New York, just down the thruway from my hometown of Syracuse. He was really funny and remembered me from when he saved my ass during my infamous malfunctioning drum riser incident back at my first gig working for Suicidal Tendencies. That story is somewhere in this book too. It's a small rock 'n' roll world, with lots of interconnected stories.

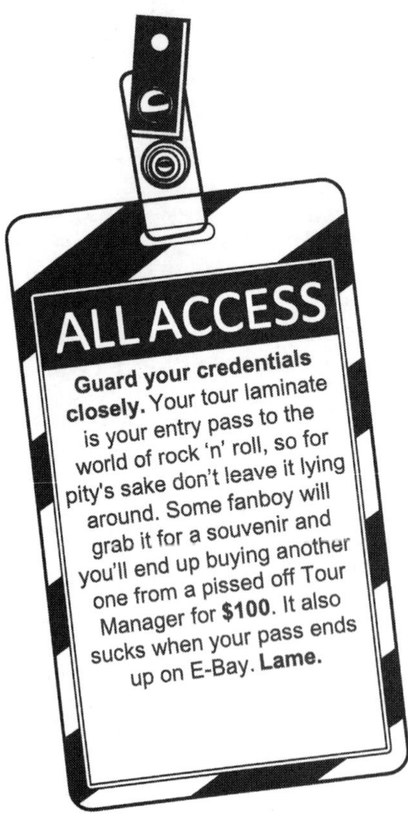

ALL ACCESS
Guard your credentials closely. Your tour laminate is your entry pass to the world of rock 'n' roll, so for pity's sake don't leave it lying around. Some fanboy will grab it for a souvenir and you'll end up buying another one from a pissed off Tour Manager for $100. It also sucks when your pass ends up on E-Bay. Lame.

It was great to see Jimmy again, and he seemed glad to have his old roadie back with him. He's always been one of the coolest guys I've ever worked for. The other band members seemed like good guys. Dave, the leader of the band, is pretty intense and definitely doesn't pull any punches. If he's got a problem with you, you'll know it right away. Marty the guitar player was quiet and kind of kept to himself. The bass player David was super cool and we hit it off right away. He's got a great personality, friendly and easy to get along with, there is absolutely no rock star BS whatsoever with that guy.

This gig would be a little different for me as far as the gear I would be working with went. Jimmy was using drum triggers now, small devices that attach to the drumheads and send a signal to a drum module or "brain" each time the drum is struck. That signal triggers an electronic drum sound. It's a great way to ensure a consistent drum sound night after night. The band was also using pre-recorded backing tracks on a few songs. A lot of bands do it. Let's say a band adds some keyboards or strings or a big vocal chorus to a song while they are recording it in the studio. In order to reproduce that sound at a live concert, they can use recorded tracks with the extra elements on it and play along with it, rather than adding an actual live keyboard player or dragging a string section out on tour to play on just that one song. The tracks have a click track built in that is sent to the drummer's monitor so he knows when to start the song and can keep time with the tracks. I would be responsible for loading the DAT tapes (Digital Audio Tape) and starting and stopping them during the shows. Megadeth was also using in-ear monitors. At the time this was somewhat new technology. Traditionally bands used small speaker cabinets onstage to hear their own vocals and instruments. This adds a lot of extra volume to the stage and can cause problems if the musicians move around on stage. They can't hear their monitor mix anymore if they move over to the other side of the stage. In-ear monitors are wireless earphones that are used in place of the traditional speaker cabinets. Each musician gets their own mix of sounds that they want to hear sent directly to their ear phones. This cuts down on a lot of extra noise onstage and the mix stays the same wherever they go onstage. It also eliminates setting up a lot of speakers and amps and saves space in the trucks. Most bands are using this technology now, but it can take some getting used to. I would also wear a set of the wireless in-ear monitors so I could hear what Jimmy was hearing and help solve any audio problems if something in his mix changed or sounded wrong.

Showtime arrived for the first gig with Megadeth. Gary and I hunkered down behind the amps next to Jimmy's drum set as the band hit the stage. After years of working for Alice Cooper, who is primarily a hard rock artist, I was a little taken aback at the ferocity of Megadeth's thrash metal style. They were out there playing fast and furious, and the crowd was going crazy. Phoenix is their adopted home town and the locals were tearing it up in the pit, headbanging and slam-dancing with reckless abandon.

The gig was pretty straight-forward, similar to the hundreds of other shows I had already done with Jimmy. But with Megadeth there was a high-tech element to much of what the roadies were doing. The drum "brain" needed to be monitored regularly to make sure the triggers were working correctly, and there were DAT tapes to play, but otherwise it was business as usual. The other backline guys on the crew were Jimmy Amason who handled Marty's guitars and Ernie Hudson who took care of Dave and David. Their jobs were made more challenging as they were tasked with doing all the "punches" during the concerts. Traditionally a guitar player will play through an amplifier setup, as well as an assortment of "outboard gear", effects processors and effects pedals. These effects allow the guitarist to change their guitar's sound to suit different songs, or change their sound for a specific section of a song. For example, a guitarist might want a fat fuzz tone sound for the rhythm parts of a song, but wants a cleaner tone for guitar solos. When the solo section of the song comes up, the guitarist can step on a foot switch and change from the rhythm tone to the solo tone, and back again. With Megadeth the guitar techs handled all the switching of guitar sounds from their tech positions on either side of the stage. They referred to this as doing "punches", and it required them to be intimately aware of the songs and all the guitar parts so they could "punch in" the correct guitar sounds at just the right moment. Megadeth's music was extremely complex, with a wide variety of guitar tones and effects, so Ernie and Jimmy had their hands full.

The Megadeth tour manager was a hilarious Brit named Steve Wood. Steve had worked with Soundgarden, KISS, Godsmack and many more. He had an epically dry British sense of humor. When it came to business he was a no-nonsense kind of guy, but when it was time to joke around he was second to none. He was a nice guy too, when we had Thanksgiving off he invited the crew to his home in New Jersey for Thanksgiving dinner. He was devoted to his son Zachary, it was really nice to get to hang out and eat turkey and pumpkin pie like people with normal lives. I had been on tour on Thanksgiving every year since 1993. Most years I ended up in a bar someplace trying to think of something to be thankful for.

Megadeth was touring to support their new album, “Risk”. It was an apt title as it was by far their most ambitious and experimental recording yet. Megadeth were riding high on the success of their previous album “Cryptic Writings”. It was a Billboard Top Ten album, and their song “Trust” hit number five on the radio charts. “Cryptic Writings” boasted a total of four top 20 radio hits and the album was also nominated for a Grammy Award. So expectations were high for the new album and tour.

The tour stage production for the “Risk” tour was equally ambitious with multiple backdrops, a massive light show and a kabuki curtain that masked the stage until showtime. Ticket sales lagged, however, as “Risk” failed to gain much traction. After starting in arenas, the venues started to get smaller and smaller as the tour went on. By the end of 1999 we were playing small theatres and clubs, which made life hard for the crew. Remember when I fell off the stage in Vienna earlier in the book trying to figure out how to fit the gear on there? That kind of thing. Many times we would pull into the parking lot of that day's venue and hope against hope that the show would be cancelled. We'd figure there's no way we can fit this band onto that stage. The old expression "Ten pounds of shit in a five pound bag" was used on an almost daily basis during this tour. The lowest point for me came when we were loading into this tiny club somewhere in the South. The bartender had a pet dog that was hanging around as we waited for the stagehands to arrive so we could start trying to fit the enormous production into this too-small venue. Just then, when our spirits were lowest, the bartender's dog walked across the stage, paused, and took a shit right at center stage. I think that about summed it up for all of us. Despite our prayers for a cancellation, we ended up doing that show, and every show on the schedule for that matter, no matter how small or literally shitty they were. Cancelled gigs mean no money, and any rock 'n' roll tour needs daily infusions of cash in order to keep going.

However, it wasn't all dog shit and bad vibes on the tour. I did end up performing with a multi-platinum heavy metal band as their offstage percussionist on this tour. One of the songs on the new Megadeth album had a tambourine part during the chorus. Halfway through the tour the band decided to add that song to the set, and of course Dave wanted to have the tambourine part in the show somehow. They thought about creating a pre-recorded backing track with the tambourine on it, but that was expensive and time-consuming for a 30 second section of one song. Jimmy came up with the idea to have me play the part. I'm a drummer, and the part was pretty simple, just steady 16th notes. For those of you who aren't drummers, trust me, it was a piece of cake, even for me. We found me a tambourine and a microphone, and for 30 seconds of every show for the remainder of the "Risk" tour I was actually in the band! Well, not really. I was actually squatting down behind the amplifier stacks playing a tambourine. I'm not sure if it even made it into the audio mix. But Dave was happy and I get to say I played in Megadeth. Sort of.

We all made it through the rest of the tour and in December the band took a short break before resuming the tour in January. They had a Millennium New Year's Eve show booked in Phoenix, but ended up deciding to cancel it. I planned to hang out in Phoenix for New Year's Eve, and since Las Vegas was our last show, rather than fly me home management had me ride with the band on their tour bus from Vegas back to Arizona.

Now, my policy as far as roadie/rockstar relations is simple: like the song says, you gotta keep 'em separated. The Megadeth guys were definitely nice enough, but being trapped with them on a locked tour bus for 8 hours on the way home from a disappointing leg of their less than stellar tour seemed like a recipe for potential disaster. Still, there was no way out of it, unless I wanted to fly myself home, which I was absolutely too cheap to do. I'd take my chances riding with the band. Marty and Jimmy flew home as they lived in California so it was just me, Dave and David on the bus from Vegas. David went to his bunk shortly after we left Sin City so it was just me and Dave hanging out in the front lounge of the tour bus. Now, Dave Mustaine is undeniably a genius guitar player. He's hailed worldwide as one of the greatest heavy metal soloists out there. He's a smart, funny, and is good at martial arts so he can kick your ass. He was the original lead guitarist in Metallica and wrote or co-wrote many of the songs on Metallica's classic debut album that catapulted the band onto the burgeoning thrash metal scene back in the early 80's. He left Metallica because of personality conflicts amid accusations of alcoholism and all-around intolerable behavior. His personal battles with drugs and alcohol are well documented. So, needless to say he's an extremely intense guy. We made some chit chat before the conversation took a somewhat dark turn. Apparently Dave wasn't very happy with the way things were going with the band. And with some of the people on the tour. I started to get uncomfortable as the discussion went on, so I excused myself at the first opportunity and scurried off to hide in my bunk before he got to me. Dave didn't seem to mind. I don't think I'm the first guy who couldn't handle hanging out with him.

During the Holiday break I was able to hang out with the Alice Cooper crew for New Year's Eve (see that story earlier in this book) before heading back to Tucson. When it was time to go back out to continue the Megadeth tour, I was totally ready. I had some crazy shit happening in my personal life that I really should have stayed home to deal with, but the siren song of the rock 'n' roll road was always too strong for me to resist, no matter who got hurt along the way or how many bridges got burned. And drinking like a fish didn't exactly help my decision making abilities back in those days. Come Hell or high water, I was on the next plane back to Roadie-Town.

Megadeth started 2000 with a string of unplugged shows and then it was back to the clubs and theatres. The acoustic shows were a lot of fun. We were doing small clubs, with mostly radio station or Megadeth fan club contest winners in the audience. Once we went back to the big shows, however, things started getting really weird. The tension between Marty and Dave was becoming obvious. Marty clearly didn't seem to be enjoying himself out there. He was still shredding his brains out onstage but other than that he was off in his own little bubble the rest of the time. The shows weren't selling like they had hoped, the "Risk" album was getting blasted by critics and metal fans alike, and the two guitar players weren't getting along, to put it mildly.

Finally things came to a head. I wasn't there, but the story is that during band discussions about the follow up album to "Risk" the plan was announced to make a more traditional speed metal album, and get back to the band's heavy metal roots. That was apparently the last straw for Marty, who quit the band on the spot. He agreed to stick around for a few weeks until a replacement could be found.

Which, given the individuals involved, was guaranteed to get weird. It was like breaking up with your girlfriend but agreeing to continue living together until the lease ran out on the apartment. What could possibly go wrong?

ALL ACCESS
Have the stuff you need close by. Make sure your spares, tools, comic books, beer cooler and everything else you'll need for the gig is within arm's reach when you need it. Also make sure you have a flashlight. It gets dark up there between songs and you don't want to fall off the stage looking for a roll of duct tape.

In Portland, Oregon, a few weeks later, Steve the tour manager gave me the news that the band was cutting back for the next leg of the tour and I would not be needed for the upcoming Asia and Europe tour dates. He was as cool as he could be about it, and let me know that I was doing a great job. There simply wasn't enough money coming in to carry a full crew and they had to cut expenses somewhere. Gaz would resume double-duty as the production manager and drum tech. I was pretty bummed out about the news. It came on a cold and rainy day in the Pacific Northwest that suited my black mood perfectly. Getting let go in January meant I would probably be sitting home without a gig until the Summer tours started up. I went for a walk in the rain to get my head together, then headed to the production office where I started making calls and looking for a new gig right away. I pissed off management by tying up the phone in the Megadeth production office every day, but what were they going to do, fire me?

Jimmy the drummer recommended the band get ahold of a guitarist named Al Pitrelli as a replacement for Marty. The two had played together in Alice Cooper's band years ago. One of the founders of the multi-platinum Trans-Siberian Orchestra symphonic rock project, Al was a tremendous guitar player and a quick learner, a skill he would need as Marty wanted out as soon as humanly possible. He was also a funny New York City guy with a wicked sense of humor. Every day Marty worked with him, showing him some of the subtleties of the Megadeth songs. Al would work on the songs with the band at soundcheck, and Marty would play the shows with Al at the side of the stage making notes. It was about as awkward a situation as you could possibly have. I can't imagine what the vibe in the dressing room or the band tour bus was like. It had to be unbearable. I was amazed nobody had cracked under the strain yet.

Finally, Marty had apparently had enough. In Vancouver, ready or not, it was show time for Megadeth's new axe man. Al took the stage that night at the Vancouver Commodore Ballroom and killed it. The band sounded solid with him in the lineup and while some Megadeth purists were outraged about Marty leaving the band, Al filled the gap like a true pro and enabled the band to stay out on tour.

My final show of the tour was in Boise, Idaho. After the gig I got drunk with Jimmy, Gaz and Ernie. I flew back to an uncertain future in Tucson the next morning with a hangover, as the rest of the gang prepared to head off to Korea and Japan to continue the Megadeth tour.

19 WISCONSIN DEATH TRIP

Imagine heavy thrash metal music with a dance beat going on underneath all the screaming and distorted guitars. That's Static X. Playing what is often referred to as alt-metal or industrial metal, their band motto was "Keep Disco Evil" and it fit their sound perfectly. They sounded exactly like Slayer if Slayer had the rhythm section from Funkadelic. Their singer Wayne had the greatest hair in the music business, it just stood straight up in the air so he kind of looked like a Q Tip or a walking exclamation point. The X men were in the middle of a marathon tour promoting their debut album "Wisconsin Death Trip" performing about 300 live shows when I got the call to come out and do my drum tech thing for them. I was grateful for the opportunity, after getting dumped from the Megadeth tour I had been worried about where my next gig would come from.

I joined up with Static-X as the new drum tech and we hit the road opening for Powerman 5000 across America, playing in mid-sized theatres and big clubs. Powerman 5000 was riding high with a platinum album sitting in the charts and two top 40 hit singles. Impressive considering they were heavy as hell and sang about rockets, robots and science fiction. Maybe the fact that their lead singer was Rob Zombie's brother helped. In any case they were a kick ass band and it would be cool to see them tearing it up every night after Static X was finished playing. This tour with

Powerman 5000 was a great opportunity for Static X to get out in front of some big crowds to promote the "Wisconsin Death Trip" album, which eventually went platinum, and a great opportunity for me to avoid reality back in the real world with a couple of months out on the road.

The drummer in the band was a guy named Ken Jay. He was a corn-fed midwestern kinda dude with a spiky blonde haircut who hit the drums like a ton of bricks. Even better, he could play those syncopated 16th note disco beats like an old school funk drummer and really made it swing when needed. I liked him right away. He had a real simple four piece drum kit and was fairly low maintenance. Static X played along to a lot of backing tracks so it was important that his in-ear monitors were on point and working right or the wheels would come off the whole thing. The guitar tech Larry operated the tape machines. Yes, more Digital Audio Tape wrangling. The backing tracks really made the band's sound as that's where all the added percussion effects and funky dance groove elements came into play.

There was a third band on the bill, another industrial influenced metal outfit from Chicago called Dope. They were fun-loving rockers who liked to party, and their band was rock solid. The Static X guys were pretty laid back, and after shows our tour bus was a little too calm for me. So when I wanted to get my party on I would always go hang out on the Dope tour bus. There was always plenty of rock action with those guys around. I even ended up roadie-ing for their drummer, Nash, for a few shows when their regular drum tech bailed.

This was yet another low budget tour. Are you sensing a pattern yet? Don't believe the hype that once a band gets a record deal and goes on tour that they have plenty of cash to spend. It just ain't true. Rock 'n' roll is still a business, and keeping expenses down and watching the bottom line is the law of the land. Once again, on this economy-minded road trip the band and crew all rode on one tour bus, with a small trailer for the gear. The crew was minimal, just me, guitar tech Larry, Bruce the sound man and Carrie the tour manager. We got a couple of guys from the touring sound crew to do monitors and lights for us. That happens a lot on tours. If a support band on the tour can't afford to bring out their own sound or lighting tech, there's almost always someone on the touring sound or lighting crew who is happy to pick up a few bucks to double dip and help out to make the shows happen. We didn't get a lot of days off, and when we did we were sharing rooms at some pretty cheap places. The opportunity to live the rock 'n' roll dream was all that I needed, so I didn't mind a bit. Anything was better than being home and facing reality at that point.

Bruce, our sound engineer, was black, and we had some pretty frank discussions about racism on tour when we were hanging out on some of those long bus rides. I can't imagine how hard it must be to work on these rock tours that are 99% white guys, and pretty much be the only black person everywhere you go, every day. I couldn't do it. No way. Bruce was an amazing sound guy, and always really nice to me, but a few times he vented and let me know how fucked up things in this country are. It helped educate me a bit and open my eyes to the realities other people are dealing with. Turns out my problems aren't the biggest ones in the world after all.

Then New Orleans happened. A day off. One of the gang took us all out to an underground vampire club near the French Quarter. There was no sign outside, it was the kind of place where you had to know somebody on the inside to get in. Kind of like Fight Club, but for people who think they're vampires. If this is your first time at Vampire Club, you HAVE to bite someone on the neck...Luckily, we had the connection and were welcomed into the world of New Orleans vampires. The basement club's clientele were exactly what you'd expect. Usually my tour crew pals are the weirdest looking people in any establishment we go to, but here we looked like members of the Young Republicans Club compared to some of the Dracula wannabe's that were hanging from the rafters in this place. The menu was loaded with vampire themed drinks, and every single one looked like blood, naturally. It was dimly lit, with creepy decor including coffins, candles, torture devices like iron maidens, and skulls everywhere. It was almost like being back on tour with Alice Cooper. I made the mistake of taking a picture of our group with my little disposable camera (this was in the days before cell phone cameras) and when the flash went off everybody got completely bent out of shape. We almost got tossed out but managed to sweet talk our way back into their good graces somehow. We ended up having a blast with the local vampire freaks and stumbled back to the tour bus in time for the ride to the next show.

The tour brought me back to some of my favorite places across America including The Roseland in NYC and the 9:30 Club in Washington, DC. But after just two months it was over and I headed back to Arizona to figure out what was next for me.

20 TONIGHT AND THE REST OF MY LIFE (OR AT LEAST THE REST OF THIS TOUR)

Nina Gordon was a singer/guitarist who had just released her debut solo album called "Tonight And The Rest Of My Life" after splitting off from the Chicago rock band Veruca Salt. I got a call to go out on the road with her for her first solo tour. This would be a major departure for me after years of working exclusively for heavy metal bands. Nina's music was eclectic, ranging from pop to rock to big beautiful ballads. For a guy who wanted nothing more than to stay out on the road as long as possible, this looked like it was going to be a fun gig.

The drummer I worked for on this trip was a Boston based guy named Steve Scully. Steve was extremely cool, very easy to work with. I probably sound like a broken record, every drummer I worked for gets described as "extremely cool and easy to work for". But it's true. I don't know if it was just dumb luck, but I never had to work for any assholes. The common denominator here is me, so maybe I just bring out the "nice guy" in people. Or at least drummers. There are plenty of horror stories about some of the personalities out there on tour, so I am grateful I got to work for so many badass drummers who also happened to be good people.

I also served as the keyboard tech on the Nina Gordon tour. Actually, all I did was set up the one keyboard every day and plug it in. Not sure if that counts as being a full-fledged keyboard “tech”. If anything had ever gone wrong with it I’m not sure what we would have done, as I wouldn’t have had the foggiest idea how to fix it. I think my go-to move would have been to hop in a taxi, head over to the closest Guitar Center music store and buy a new one.

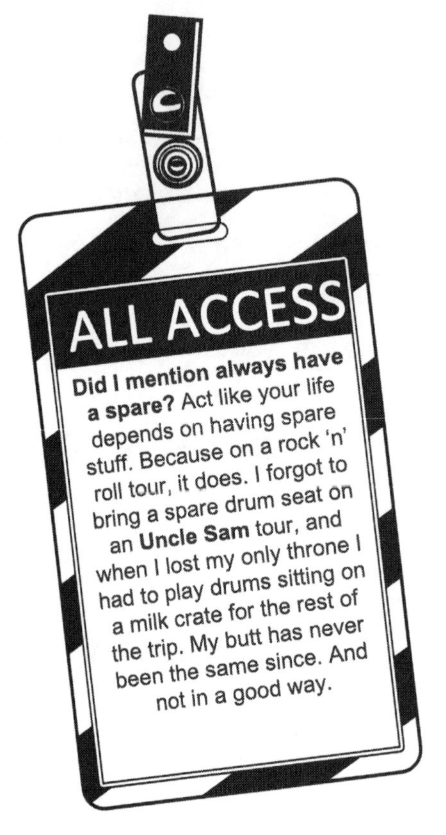

ALL ACCESS
Did I mention always have a spare? Act like your life depends on having spare stuff. Because on a rock ‘n’ roll tour, it does. I forgot to bring a spare drum seat on an **Uncle Sam** tour, and when I lost my only throne I had to play drums sitting on a milk crate for the rest of the trip. My butt has never been the same since. And not in a good way.

Talk about a low stress working environment. The band and crew were riding on one bus together, and we were traveling light with a skeleton crew: just me, a guitar tech, and the tour manager/ sound engineer. Nina’s album was doing well on Top 40 radio and she was booked into some big places. We did our fair share of dive bars too, as it can be take-it-or-leave-it for new artists trying to break out. She had some major success with Veruca Salt so she was at least fairly well known, but trying to launch her new solo project meant starting over at the bottom in many ways.

The band were all solid players and easy to work for. Nina’s boyfriend Stacy would stop out to hang out on the tour for a few days at a stretch every once in a while. He played drums on Nina's solo album but was on tour with his own band as the lead singer in American Hi Fi. Nina and her backup band liked to have a glass of whiskey before the shows, presumably for stage fright. That's what I was using it for, anyway. She was cool about sharing.

New Year's Eve brought the tour to an end with a show in Nina's home town of Chicago. It was a crazy way to end a crazy year. So much had changed for me in the past 365 days. The gig was packed and she tore the roof off the place. We finished up before midnight, so after the show Nina invited us all to come and party at her place. That was pretty cool of her. She had a nice place, great food and cool music. I was pretty blown away that she would invite us all into her home. That says a lot about what kind of person Nina is. We rang in 2001 together and headed into the new year. There was no way to be sure what it would hold.

But wait! There's more! I got the call to do another gig with Nina shortly after I got home from the New year's Eve gig. She was booked to play at an MTV fashion show event, playing on live TV on a beach in Miami, Florida. We were going to be doing this on a shoestring budget, so I was the only tech they were flying in. Somehow after only two months I had become the lynchpin of Nina Gordon's tour crew. What can I say? I'm obviously an invaluable asset to any rock show. Nina's management asked me if I knew any local guitar techs that might be available to do this one-off show for us. Did I ever. That's how my old touring buddy Ken Barr got in on the gig. He lived in Florida so travel expenses would be minimal, and he was sure to do a great job. It was great to see him and it felt good to do him a solid by getting him a nice pay day. He did his usual amazingly professional job. Some folks can't do it any other way.

After the MTV show Nina took us all out on the town in downtown Miami. Normally a roadie's best policy is to stay away from the band when we aren't working. It's too easy to have one or two drinks too many, say or do something stupid, and end up regretting it or worse yet getting sent home for it. But Miami is a great place to party, and the record company was paying. At the time Nina was a pretty big star with a hit album, and Miami is a big town with a lot of celebrities.

Miami also has a lot of possibilities, and eventually we were hanging out with Alex Rodriguez and some other pro baseball players at this huge dance club. A - Rod had just signed the biggest contract in sports history with the Texas Rangers for $252 million. I don't dance, but I do drink, and the vibe in this place was terrific. Another rock 'n' roll show, another party. Another flight back to Arizona with a hangover.

21 YOU WANTED THE BEST (BUT THIS DRUM ROADIE IS ALL WE HAD)

Virtually everyone was a KISS fan in the 70's, including me. It was hard not to be a fan, since as a kid who grew up interested in fantasy, science fiction, sports and sex, KISS were the living embodiment all those elements. Imagine Dungeons and Dragons with electric guitars! They walked the Earth like some sort of rock 'n' roll Tyrannosaurus Rex during the Jurassic Period of the late 70's, proudly flying their freak flag and getting rich doing it. They were everything a chubby teen ager in the boondocks like me wanted to be. They were rich and famous. They played rock 'n' roll music, had great hair and cool clothes. They even had sex with girls. Frequently! They were larger than life, and their songs were the soundtrack as I tried to find my way through suburban American pubescence.

Punk rock was born at the end of that decade, and it (and it's bastard child thrash metal) soon won my affections away from KISS and their hair rock ilk. Hard rocking guitar heroes would continue to peddle their wares throughout the 80's to great success, but the world had moved on by that point. Eventually Kurt Cobain would lead his flannel clad tribe out of the wilderness of the Pacific Northwest (quite literally a wilderness - have you ever been to Boise?) and drive a stake through the heart of hair metal once and for all.

Fast forward to the beginning of 2001. KISS were on their "Farewell Tour" with the original lineup of Gene Simmons, Paul Stanley, Ace Frehley and Peter Criss when Peter abruptly left the band in the middle of the world tour. The story goes that he wanted more money than Gene and Paul were willing to pay. I'm not sure what the deal was, but with the end of the tour looming KISS needed a drummer for the Japanese and Australian dates. And they needed one quick.

Eric Singer was the logical choice to fill the newly vacant drum throne. He had played in the band from 1991 until 1996, he already knew most of the songs, he got along with the other guys in the band, and most importantly, was available immediately, as he had just completed Alice Cooper's "Brutal Planet" world tour.

Eric reached out to me to see if I'd be interested in teching for him on these KISS shows. He let me know right off the bat that working for KISS would be vastly different from working for the other bands I had toured with. The KISS shows would be much bigger than anything I had worked before, with the accompanying pressure. We would be headlining venues like Japan's famous Tokyo Dome and the Superdome in Sydney. Also, the rest of the crew had been on tour together for an entire year, so they had a solid group dynamic already in place. I would be "the new guy" in a big way, and fitting in seamlessly would be both a priority and a challenge.

Also, Eric sang backup vocals on almost every KISS song. Naturally this was not a simple matter of putting up a vocal microphone on a boom mic stand and letting him sing his little heart out. If you've ever seen Eric play, you know he's extremely visual. He does lots of stick twirling and tossing, as well as a full complement of arm swinging, hair flipping, and other assorted rock 'n' roll gyrations. Part of the gig as drum roadie for Eric with KISS was operating his specially designed boom microphone stand.

Eric had a custom built microphone stand that facilitates his simultaneous drumming and vocalizing. It's just like a regular microphone stand except that it swivels at its base, so his faithful drum roadie can maneuver it. My job was to swing the microphone in close enough for him to sing into whenever needed, and swing the mic back out to give him room for his stick-twirling, arm-waving drumming theatrics the rest of the time. This entailed me being intimately familiar with the KISS songs so I could have the mic properly positioned at the right times. Part of my job was also to not hit him in the eye or break his teeth with a mis-timed swing of the microphone stand.

It was with mixed emotions that I took the job as Eric's drum tech for the KISS tour. I had just finished up the tour with Nina Gordon, and needed a new gig. Working for a legendary band like KISS was too much for me to pass up, no matter how challenging the gig was going to be. This would be a completely new experience, an opportunity to take my roadie game to the next level. Plus, after a lifetime of dreaming of getting to this point, being a roadie was all I wanted to do. Hell, by now it was all I knew how to do. And if there's one thing I had learned over the years, it's that you never turn down work in this business. People forget you very quickly when you say no to a job offer.

Luckily for me, since Eric had been out of the band for several years, rehearsals were scheduled to prep for the tour. That would at least give me a chance to meet the other guys in the band, get a little face time with their management, and most importantly, break the ice with the other backline techs that I would be working very closely with every day on the tour. I already knew a few faces when I arrived at the rehearsals in Los Angeles. I had worked with Spike, Gene Simmons' bass tech, on an Alice Cooper tour not too long ago. We had gotten along well while we were out on the road working with the Coop, and he was sort of the "elder statesman" of the KISS backline crew. Having Spike in my corner would make my life a lot easier in the KISS roadie camp.

The first day the band was working on the set list, getting their sounds together and jamming on some tunes. It was Eric's first time playing in KISS with their original lead guitarist Ace Frehley, aside from some brief "KISS Unplugged" sessions, so there was a bit of a "getting-to-know-you" phase. This worked to my advantage because I needed time to chart out the songs and take notes on when Eric would be singing. I'd need to know the songs inside and out in order to operate that mic stand properly. Even though I was busy feverishly charting songs and prepping Eric's tour gear I found a little time to soak in the incredible experience

I was having. KISS was right there in front of me rocking out. And I was in the same room! I would be roadie-ing for them! In Japan! Ace Frehley was standing 4 feet away from me playing his rocket launcher guitar...the one with the mirrored pickguard and built-in smoke bombs! It would have been a dream come true for my 12 year old self.

This was no time to get starstruck. Any rock 'n' roll fan would be digging this scene big time, but I did my best to keep my mind on my work. KISS were true professionals in every sense of the word, and I'd be out of a job quickly if I wasn't 100% focused. I especially didn't want to let Eric down. As big an opportunity as this was for me, it was a major career opportunity for him. I wanted to do everything I could to make this gig go smoothly for us both.

Staying out of the way and flying under the radar was a priority at rehearsals. Gene and Paul are rock 'n' roll visionaries, so don't piss them off. Despite my best efforts to avoid screwing up, I had a close call with Gene. While the band was playing a song he caught my attention, pointed at the empty Snapple bottle on his amp, and made some sort of hand gesture that might have meant either "Please get me another one of these," or "Steal second base on the next pitch". I was guilty of violating Roadie Rule #1: NEVER make eye contact with the band. Frantically I looked around for Spike to translate Gene's request, but he was nowhere to be seen. Good lord man, this is no time for a bathroom break! I ran into the kitchen area, grabbed another Snapple, ran it back to the practice room and put it on Gene's amp. He looked at it, looked at me, and started shaking his head and making more incomprehensible hand gestures while mouthing words at me. They looked like unhappy words, but I couldn't hear them because KISS was playing in the same room. Loudly. I broke into a cold sweat. I had absolutely no idea what he wanted. The God Of Thunder (and Rock 'n' Roll) had me in his sights! I began rehearsing my apology to Eric just in case Gene fired me on the spot like Donald Trump on "The Apprentice". Suddenly, Spike returned! The day was saved! The correct Snapple was procured! I scurried out of the rehearsal room and hid in the bathroom.

I was amped up as I got on the plane to Japan. I had been there several times before with other bands and tours, but this time was really different. There were so many unknowns looming, it kind of felt like my first time all over again. It was like this was the first chapter of a new stage of my touring career. The whole vibe with KISS was so different for me. It was scary and exhilarating at the same time. Luckily drinks are still free on International flights.

Arriving at Yokohama airport and clearing Customs was a blur of jet lag, explaining to baggage control why I needed so many dangerous looking tools, and a Business Class champagne hangover. When I was met at the gate by a limo driver holding a sign with my name on it, I knew I had reached the roadie version of the Big Time at last.

Day one in Yokohama was load-in and setup. With KISS you didn't really get days off because the production was so enormous we needed to start loading in the day before in most cities. I was glad to have an extra day to get my hands on the gear and get my head wrapped around what life on a KISS tour was going to be like. Eric had brought out some new gear for this tour. When the word got out that he was going to be back in KISS, wearing the makeup and completing their historic Farewell Tour, drum gear suppliers were eager to get on board and several of them had hooked him up with a bunch of new toys to play with. Eric was using these new high tech cymbal stand toppers for this tour. They used a tiny locking nut to hold the cymbal exactly where he wanted it. You adjusted them with a similarly tiny Allen key. Normally a cymbal is held in place on its cymbal stand with a traditional wing nut. The problem was, Eric Singer hits the drums hard. Really hard. His cymbal holders were constantly loosening up until the cymbals would start to flop around wildly and become impossible for him to hit. The first solution Eric came up with was a liberal application of a product called Loc-Tite. It's a liquid threadlocker that gums up the threads on the wing nuts so they don't work their way loose. The only drawback is that they become pretty difficult to get off even if you want them to. Eric pitched this idea to me early in our working relationship.

"J Mann, remember, when you're putting the cymbals on, be sure to use Loc-Tite," he informed me at some long-forgotten Alice Cooper rehearsal back in 1997. "Sure thing, you bet, no worries, I'm on it, you can count on me," I replied and promptly forgot about it. Fast forward to the first gig with Eric. He's up there bashing away at the drums like they owe him money, Alice Cooper is out there waving a sword around or whatever it is he does when he's being Alice Cooper and I'm sitting there watching it all happening and thinking, "Gee, this Eric Singer guy seems all right." Suddenly, cymbal wingnuts start popping off. Cymbals are flying all over the place as Eric is literally beating his drum set to pieces. I leap to my feet and start running around the stage frantically trying to put the wayward wing nuts back on without getting hit by flying drumsticks or stabbed to death by Alice Cooper. I managed to get through the gig somehow, but I learned my lesson.

Life on a KISS tour was BIG. Yokohama arena holds 17,000 people and KISS was playing two nights there. When I arrived at the arena on that first setup day, the carpenter's crcw was finishing up building the stage. KISS carries their own stage and crew of techs to set it up so everything is exactly the same every show. Some tours will source the stage decking locally, but not these guys. Everything about the KISS organization was done right. That created some pressure for the crew, as the bar for acceptable performance was set pretty high.

Just like a drum set, a drum roadie's job consists of many different parts. Cleaning cymbals, changing drum heads, marking gear so I could set things up the same way every night, soon enough I was ready for Eric to show up. The roadies whiled away the time as we waited for the band to arrive at soundcheck by playing "Classic Rock Name That Band". Each tech on the tour was issued a walkie talkie, and we all shared a common communications channel. This enabled management or the band to locate someone quickly no matter where they were at the venue. It also enabled us to goof around by trying to top each other by coming up with the most obscure rock band names we could think of. One after another, roadies would invoke the name of a long-defunct group. Spike was the judge of our little trivia game. He had a near-encyclopedic knowledge of rock 'n' roll, so if he approved the band you had suggested you stayed in the game. If he hadn't heard of the hair band you had invoked, too bad, so sad...you were out.

Finally the band arrived and it was back to work for soundcheck.

Meeting Ace Frehley was like meeting Abraham Lincoln, if Abraham Lincoln played a Les Paul guitar that shot fire out of the end. The original lead guitarist for KISS, his original guitar style - equal parts parts soulful blues and hard hitting rock 'n' roll shredding - became a vital part of the band's trademark sound. But working with him could be challenging, as he is an eccentric guy, to say the least! He had brought a huge remote control helicopter out on the tour with him. This was in the days before drones, and this thing was big, dangerous and hard to control. He would try to put a camera on it and get it to fly around the arenas the band was playing in to take aerial photographs. I'm not sure if the photos ever worked out, but I did see it crash several times. Ace was still an amazing player when he was in the zone on this tour. He had been through a lot during his rock 'n' roll career. Legend has it he was once electrocuted on stage during a KISS concert in Lakeland, Florida when he accidentally grabbed a metal handrail and inadvertently completed an electrical circuit, delivering a near-fatal jolt that knocked him unconscious. He later wrote the song "Shock Me" about the incident. After leaving KISS back in 1982 he had his share of troubles including an infamous car wreck where he totaled a DeLorean after a police chase. He is definitely one of rock's most memorable characters.

Finally, it was time. My first KISS show as an official KISS roadie. Another rock 'n' roll dream about to come true! The Yokohama arena was completely sold out, and as the KISS Army poured in I was trying to stay calm. I double-checked the drum set. Everything was good to go. The band had pulled out all the stops for their return to Japan. There were gigantic inflatable replicas of each band member standing tall on either side of the stage. Paul's codpiece seemed a little over-stuffed, but otherwise they were pretty good likenesses considering they were 40 feet tall and made of the same shit as the Goodyear Blimp. The audience's view of the stage was masked by a huge Kabuki curtain stretched across the front.

The stage production for the Farewell Tour was mind-blowing. It featured staircases for the band to run around on, walls of amplifier cabinets and the iconic enormous lighted KISS sign at the back of the stage. There were video screens so everyone in the stadium could feel like they had front row seats. The drum riser was actually suspended from the ceiling so it could rise and lower during the show. There was a second, smaller stage section that also hung down from the ceiling and went up and down on chain motors for the three other band members to ride down from the ceiling on. At least their flying stage section had seat belts to keep them from toppling off, Eric was on his own on the floating drum riser with only gravity to keep him in place. And there were two massive scissor-lifts that would lift Gene, Paul and Ace into the sky as well. Along with an immense light show and a virtual military-grade arsenal of explosives, sparklers, flame-throwers and concussion mortars, this stage show was bigger than anything I had ever seen, let alone been part of.

ALL ACCESS
Don't drink and roadie. The temptation to have a drink during a show can be hard to resist. **Rock 'n' Roll** is all about the party life, right? Well, that's true. But after a fellow roadie (no names but his initials are KB) threatened to break my ankle if I kept boozing during loadout I decided to clean up my act. At least until the truck was loaded.

As the band's intro tape rolled Eric appeared at the back of the stage, escorted by the stage manager, Ragman. Eric climbed up onto the drum riser and I waved goodbye as he rose up out of sight. The other members of KISS took their places on the second floating platform and disappeared into the rafters. I held my breath. When the intro music hit its peak, everything seemed to happen at once. I could hear Eric count off the first song on his hi-hat cymbals from high overhead, then an enormous pyro blast went off as the Kabuki curtain dropped and the band began coming down from the ceiling of the arena. It looked like a pair of spaceships crash-landing as smoke bombs and fog machines pumped from the bottoms to the platforms like jet engines. I watched as the drum riser got closer and finally touched down on the drum platform. I had been warned to stay clear of the drum riser whenever it was coming down, as any malfunction of the chain motors that carried it up and down could result in a deadly accident. Once it was safely down I scrambled up the stairs at the back of the riser and took my position crouched down to Eric's left. As the opening song, "Detroit Rock City", hit the chorus I swung the vocal microphone in. Eric sang his part and then out went the microphone, right on cue. Eric gave me a quick grin. So far, so good.

The show passed in a blur. I was kept busy the whole time. Between operating the vocal microphone, serving up cold drinks between songs, and climbing off the riser every time it made a return trip to the heavens I didn't have much free time. I had to remember that if the drummer is wearing full-face stage makeup you need to put a straw in his water bottle so he won't spoil his face paint. I even had a headset radio with a direct line to the monitor board so I could relay Eric's audio requests to the monitor engineer without having to make the trek over to the side of the stage.

A favorite part of the show was when Spike snuck out onto the stage during Gene's bass solo to clip a pair of cables onto his costume just as The Demon is spitting blood all over the place. I'm pretty sure Spike wore an actual Haz-Mat suit to protect him from the flying spit, sweat, blood and other assorted expectorants that Gene emits somewhat freely during the concerts. Suddenly the wires engage and Gene flies 30 feet straight up into the air like some kind of bat and lands on a platform on top of the lighting truss. He sings "I Love It Loud" from up there and Yokohama goes berserk. I wasn't expecting that gag. Not to be outdone Paul rode a cable out to a mini-stage in the middle of the arena to sing "Love Gun", giving everybody in the cheap seats a front-row seat for one song only! Before I knew it the show was over and it was back to the hotel. No load out since we had a second show the following night.

Doing multiple shows at the same venue is great because everything is pretty much ready to go the next day. We did have to sweep up loads of confetti scattered all over everything from the night before, but otherwise day two was a breeze. The band showed up just before the show, no sound check this time. Intro tape, kabuki drop, pyro blast and we were off to the races for another night.

After the show the lights came up and the real work began. Load out is a pretty critical part of the day. KISS has so much gear that it takes coordinated effort by everybody on the crew as well as the local hands to get it done right. On a good night it runs like clockwork and the trucks seem to load themselves. Everything is ready when we open the trucks again at the next show if we get it right. I had a few problems and ended up taking some heat from Ragman. Remember those fancy new cymbal holders Eric brought out for this tour? Turns out those gadgets are great at keeping cymbals on, but take forever to get the cymbals off. I was fussing around with those damn things for what seemed like forever and I ended up holding up load out. We all worked through it and got it done, but it definitely wasn't the way I wanted my first load out with my new crew to go.

The KISS crew was big, by far the biggest crew I had ever been on. Besides the usual backline, sound and lighting techs KISS had a wardrobe department, video, special effects, pyro, carpenters and a staging crew on the road with them as well. Paul Stanley's guitar tech was a younger guy named Fluffy, and Ace's tech Larry was a laid back fellow from Atlanta. Larry had worked on some big tours like Kid Rock, and was down to earth and easy going. We hit it off pretty well right away. The production manager was a veteran of many rock tours named Patrick. Patrick had toured with Thin Lizzy and Van Halen back in the 70's and he really knew his stuff, he took great care of our crew.

I was never quite sure how the other guys on the crew felt about me. Fitting in with all the new faces on the KISS tour was a bit of a challenge for me. And on a touring crew this big, odds are that I would experience a conflict or two. I'm pretty much a gregarious, get-along kinda guy. But like I said, these guys had all been together, living together, working together, and traveling all over the world together for a full calendar year before I dropped in on their happy little family. Everybody treated me well for the most part, but with a crew that large there are bound to be personality conflicts.

This was the first tour I had ever done that had pyrotechnics in the show. And not just a few sparklers. KISS carried a full crew of pyro techs, and those guys were the busiest dudes on the crew. To say there are a lot of explosions in a KISS show would be an understatement. One lesson I learned on a tour with pryo was always tell the production manager if the drummer comes up with any crazy ideas involving flaming drumsticks.

After a few shows Eric came up with the idea to bring back his flaming drum stick drum solo. He had done this stunt before when I was working with him on an Alice Cooper tour. It was pretty simple: I would soak a pair of drum mallets in a jar of lighter fluid before the show. During the drum solo Eric would toss his regular drum sticks out to the crowd. Then while playing a pattern on his bass drums, he'd put his hands behind his back. I would slip the soaked mallets into his waiting hands, light them and tap him on the back to let him know when they had caught. He'd then bring them out and play the rest of the solo with the flaming sticks. It was a pretty good gag, people seemed to dig it, and it rarely went wrong. I would stay close by with a lighter and if one of the sticks ever went out I could reach up and relight it for Eric while he played with the other one.

However, when Eric brought the idea to me it never dawned on me to notify the pyro guys or the production manager, Patrick. I just went about the process of getting the stuff needed and the logistics of incorporating it into the gig. When Patrick caught wind of it he dropped the hammer on me pretty hard. I totally had it coming. Failing to keep him in the loop could really have caused some major problems for the whole tour. After checking with the pyro guys we were able to move forward with the flaming sticks, but I really could have caused some dangerous problems if I had just went for it like I was planning to. That drum riser was loaded with various explosives and pyro charges and I could easily have accidentally set something off at the wrong time. The shit KISS uses onstage can kill somebody if it isn't used right. That was actually a really close call.

Doing a tour with all this crazy production and special effects presented other unique challenges as well. The drum riser wasn't just a platform for the drum set on a tour like this. It also housed an assortment of lighting and pyrotechnics as well. When the riser rose into the air (or came down to the stage from the overhead truss) fog, smoke bombs and pyro charges would shoot from the bottom of it, and there were lights mounted on the bottom of the riser as well. As a result, the riser spent a lot of time suspended in the air over the stage so the crew could work on the underside of it to load pyro charges, adjust the lights and perform other maintenance tasks.

I, of course, had my own business to conduct on the TOP of the riser. I'd be sitting behind the drum set, changing heads, cleaning cymbals, or doing other drum roadie stuff when suddenly the riser would start to rise up into the air.

The riser would go up so high I couldn't get down, so I was constantly getting stranded up there as the pyro guys worked on the bottom of the riser. I think they might have been doing it on purpose just to see me peering down forlornly from on high as they pretended to do something to the riser.

We had a day off as we traveled from Fukuoka to Nagoya. Some of us stopped to visit the Atomic Dome Museum in Hiroshima on the way. It is also known as the Hiroshima Peace Museum. Originally built in 1915 as an exhibition hall, it was the only building left standing near ground zero in Hiroshima after the atomic bomb. The museum is in the middle of this beautiful green park, so the contents inside are somewhat jarring. It has exhibits and artifacts showing the devastation caused by America's 1945 atomic bomb attack. The exhibit that really got to me was a section of stone wall with a human outline actually burned into it, indicating just how fast and intensely hot the atomic explosion was. Can you even imagine being caught in that hell? Among the other exhibits were a melted tricycle that belonged to a young child killed by the atomic blast, photos of the survivors and victims of radiation poisoning, and the "Flame of Peace", an eternal flame that has become a symbol of the anti-nuclear weapons movement around the world. The day we visited was rainy and overcast and it suited the somber tone of the place perfectly. The underlying message was hope that something so horrible would never happen again. It wasn't easy to see some of the sights there, but I am glad I went.

Another amazing opportunity was visiting the Kyoto temples. Patrick and his wife Diane, who was on the tour as a production assistant, took some of us roadies on a trip to Kyoto on a day off to tour their incredible temples. Kyoto was the first capital of Japan and it has some of the most amazing Shinto shrines and Buddhist temples in the world. We saw Nijo Castle, Heian Shrine and many more ancient buildings. They have been kept up beautifully and are fully functioning as religious sites. We had to remove our shoes and be extremely quiet while visiting the temples, which is not easy for a gaggle of rock roadies on the loose in Japan. I think we did okay, hopefully the Buddha will forgive us for any outbursts. There were so many amazing places to visit I started to lose track. One beautiful intricately adorned temple started to merge with the next in my mind. Patrick set a torrid pace, approaching a day of sight-seeing like he approached a major concert tour - get in, get it done, and move on! It was an unforgettable experience and Kyoto is one place I would definitely love to visit again.

By this time in my roadie career, I was actively trying to save money on the road. I had started dating an awesome lady back in Arizona and was starting to think about a possible future after the road. You need money for a future. Japan was notoriously expensive in those days, so we received double per diems. I tried to make mine stretch as far as I could. We had a lot of travel days and days off, which can really eat into your wallet. Japanese hotel rooms have boiling water spigots in the rooms for making tea, so I would buy cheap ramen noodle bowls at the convenience stores near the hotels and cook them in my room for an inexpensive meal. I was able to bring home a lot of my PDs that way.

Soon enough it was time to leave Japan and move on to Australia. I was hoping to have a chance visit my old friends the fairy penguins. We arrived in Perth on Australia's West coast. I had toured down under before but had never been to Perth. KISS put us up at a beautiful hotel right on this amazing white sand beach. I walked down to the ocean and it was literally a breathtaking sight. I have never seen water so blue and beautiful, it felt like I could see God right there in the Indian Ocean.

Imagine seeing Sydney Harbor from the top of its world-famous bridge. Been there, done that. Yup, we climbed that thing! On a night off in Sydney a few of the crew went on the Sydney Harbor Bridge climbing tour. They outfitted us with climbing suits and harnesses before we started, attached to a continuous railing, so you can't fall off. Even if you tried to jump over the edge, you couldn't do it. Apparently a few people have tried to commit suicide while on the climbing tour. So it's been rendered completely safe, but still exhilarating to be that high up. We went at night and the view of the city lights was tremendous. I felt so alive up there, so lucky to be literally on top of a bridge at the bottom of the world.

The Australian shows were incredible, Australia has always been one of my favorite places to visit because of the friendly people. KISS added a few songs to the set list especially for their Australian crowds. "Shandi" had been a huge hit in Australia but no place else on Earth, so they dusted it off for the crowds down under. My last gig with KISS on this tour was at Carrara Stadium in Gold Coast. We had a couple of days off before the show which was a good thing because it was an outdoor show, and we needed to reconfigure some of the special effects for the outdoor set up. The show was a blast, the band seemed to be having a good time playing with Eric for the entire tour but tonight they really cut loose and even jammed on a few songs. Ace just started screwing around and playing songs that weren't on the set list and Eric and the other guys would join in! They did little bits of KISS classics like "Parasite", "New York Groove" with Ace singing lead vocals, "She", "Makin' Love" and the classic "Strutter". I was geeking out hard over it and the crowd ate it up. It was a great way to end the tour. By this time I had my load out dialed in and we got out of there in good time. The last show of any tour is hectic because the crew has to get all the gear labelled to be shipped home

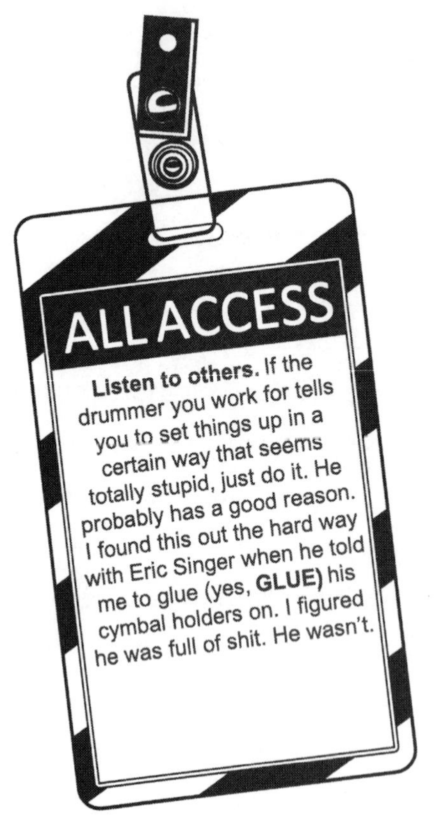

ALL ACCESS
Listen to others. If the drummer you work for tells you to set things up in a certain way that seems totally stupid, just do it. He probably has a good reason. I found this out the hard way with Eric Singer when he told me to glue (yes, GLUE) his cymbal holders on. I figured he was full of shit. He wasn't.

afterwards and coordinate everything with the shipping companies. It was a long night but I felt so relieved it had gone so well, and gratified by the whole experience that I hardly felt tired at all. Back at the hotel I had a few drinks with the guys. The next day we all went our separate ways like always. No looking back. There's always the next gig to find, another plane to catch, and one more road to travel.

Driving home from the airport back in Arizona I had a message on my cell phone from Eric. "J Mann, it's Eric. Hope you got home safe, I didn't get to see you after the show. I wanted to say thanks, you really knocked it out of the park on this one, and I appreciate it. Peace."

You're welcome, Eric. It was the gig of a lifetime for me.

KISS booked a few more one-off shows after the Japan/Australia tour ended, including a live performance at the closing ceremonies of the 2002 Winter Olympics in Salt Lake City, Utah. Getting to be a part of the Olympics was an amazing experience. But like everything KISS does it wasn't quite what you'd expect. Arriving at the Olympic Stadium we were herded through a variety of security checkpoints before being issued our credentials and identification cards. There were just two roadies on this gig, me and their warehouse manager. KISS has an enormous warehouse in Los Angeles where they store...well, everything. It has their old costumes, stage set pieces, musical instruments, and road cases. It's like Disneyland for KISS fanatics. But since the band wasn't going to be performing, just lip-syncing to their iconic song "Rock & Roll All Nite", we didn't really need a full road crew.

The main thing was that the band had their costumes, make-up cases, and some sort of prop guitars and drums to pretend to play while they sang. Eric even had me stuff the drum shells with styrofoam packing peanuts so they wouldn't make any sound when he hit them.

KISS would be performing on a huge parade float being driven around an ice skating rink as they played. Now, this was no ordinary parade float. It came equipped with an array of pyrotechnic charges that would shoot explosives and sparks all around the arena. It was such an unusual place to be rocking out that the band arranged for a "boot rehearsal". What on earth is a "boot rehearsal", you ask? It's where the band practices walking around on the parade float in their famous platform boots during soundcheck in order to make sure they don't fall off the god damned thing as it rolls around the ice.

That night the Olympic stadium was packed with fans, celebrities and Olympic athletes as KISS prepared to take the stage. I was ready to hand Eric his sticks and get out of the way when Gene beckoned to me. Decked out in his full Demon makeup and costume, the God Of Thunder pointed at his infamous axe-shaped bass guitar and asked me to give it to him. I sheepishly picked it up and held the thing out to him.

He held his arms out and glared at me as he waited for me to put the giant guitar on him. I realized that with the elaborate shoulder pads, spikes, bat wings and other assorted protuberances attached to his stage costume Gene would have a hell of a time putting on his own guitar. Of course I'm about a foot shorter than Gene in street shoes, let alone when he's wearing those famous platform boots! I struggled to get the guitar strap over his head without screwing up his iconic topknot or smear his face paint. It wasn't going well, and as the stage manager started counting down the seconds until KISS was supposed to start playing my life flashed before my eyes. At last I saw that there was a metal guide attached to Gene's costume to hold the guitar strap in place. Finally I was able to get the thing attached to him adequately, and off he stomped to make rock 'n' roll history.

In what may well be a display of instant karma, the stage/float caught fire during the band's performance as sparks from the pyro charges ignited a few sections of their rolling stage. Luckily the song is only three minutes long and the Salt Lake City fire department was able to wait until the band was finished to extinguish the flames. It actually looked pretty cool on TV.

KISS also played a private concert in Montego Bay, Jamaica. They brought out the full road crew for this one-off performance: sound, lighting, video, pyro, the whole shebang. Rumor has it that the event was part of a week-long birthday celebration for a Russian billionaire. All the roadies cared about was that we were staying at a clothing-optional resort packed with Russian super models. The show took place on a golf course where the faithful crew dutifully built the enormous KISS stage. As show time approached tension rose backstage as lead guitarist Ace Frehley was nowhere to be found. Finally it was showtime, and still no Ace. With no choice other than to cancel the show (and if you think any rock 'n' roll band is going to walk away from a payday you're crazy), tour manager Tommy Thayer put on the Space Ace makeup and costume and took Ace's spot in the band for the night. Tommy had previously played in a KISS tribute band for years and probably knew Ace's guitar parts better than Ace did at this point. The show went off without a hitch, with KISS putting on their full arena rock concert for a few hundred of the birthday boy's friends and family. Nobody seemed to notice that Ace was missing, but the internet trolls went crazy when they found out about it after the fact.

Tommy Thayer ended up eventually becoming an actual full-blown member of KISS after Ace left the band again following the farewell tour. Talk about a dream come true! Tommy's a great guy, a hell of a guitar player and I am totally happy it worked out for him the way it did. It's like they say, in America if you work hard and follow your dream, anything is possible. Especially if the guy who has the job you want flakes out and doesn't show up for work.

KISS had one more oddball show coming up and this one was the weirdest one yet. The band was booked to play at a Lane Bryant fashion show in New York City. The plus-sized clothing store chain was putting on a "Rock The Runway" event (featuring a lingerie fashion show) and hired KISS to provide the music. I guess it actually makes sense now that I think about it. Any band that has literally been singing the praises of women for their entire career is the perfect band to provide the soundtrack for an event such as this one! The band played about five songs as the lingerie models strutted their stuff on a specially designed runway stage in front of the band. I even got to meet Anna Nicole Smith. Yet another dream comes true, thanks to the power of rock 'n' roll.

22 IDLE HANDS ARE THE DEVIL'S PLAYGROUND

Being a rock roadie, especially at the higher levels of international touring, is hard work. There's no question about that. The bands and managers expect more from the people who work for them, especially since those high level road guys get paid damn well. There is a lot of money on the line, and with it comes a lot of pressure to perform at the highest level. The travel is grueling, the working conditions change constantly and you never know where your next gig will come from when a tour ends. There's no health insurance or company benefits when you are your own boss.

Naturally, roadies need to blow off steam once in a while when they're on tour. Plenty of folks on the road like to relax after the show is over, or on days off, with a few drinks or their favorite substance. Some like to play practical jokes or pranks on each other to break the tension. It's natural, it's healthy and on some of the tours I've been on it's downright necessary. There is a lot of downtime on tour. It's a constant game of "hurry up & wait." We drive all night to get to the next gig, then wait for the venue to open up so we can load in. We rush through load-in and set-up, then wait for the band to get there to sound-check. We hustle to get everything ready in time for the doors to open, then wait till show time. One way to blow off steam is drinking. During my touring years I could frequently be found hanging around at the hotel bar anytime we were lucky enough to get a day off that wasn't a travel day. Some guys liked to go out and find a cool club on a night off, or cab over to the local strip club. I preferred the elegant simplicity of the hotel bar. At the end of the night all I had to do was charge the drinks to my room, stagger to the elevator, try to find my room, and pass out. On one Christmas tour with Alice Cooper we played several shows in Michigan, leading up to a New Year's Eve show at Joe Louis Arena in Detroit. We stayed at the Detroit airport hotel for the whole week, and just rode the tour bus out to the different shows, returning "home" each night afterwards. Needless to say I logged a lot of hours at that Detroit hotel bar. I got to know the bar staff pretty well, as I am a talkative, gregarious fellow, especially when I'm drunk, and I strongly believe in over-tipping. Especially when I'm drunk.

We returned to the hotel very late after a show in Grand Rapids and headed for the familiar environs of the hotel bar, only to discover that it was closed. I was outraged. Also thirsty. I loudly voiced my displeasure at this state of affairs. "You gotta be kidding me!" I roared at the frightened desk clerk as I pounded my fist on the counter. "We book 30 rooms here for a friggin' week, we've been in that bar every night spending tons of money, and you people can't keep the goddam place open for an hour so we can spend some MORE money here? This is unbelievable!" Following this tirade I threw up my hands and dejectedly went up to my room, trying to figure out where I could go to get a drink at that hour. Suddenly my hotel room phone rang. It was Ken, our guitar tech.

“J Mann! The hotel manager heard you complaining, and they’re going to open up the bar for us. Get down here fast!”

The squeaky wheel does indeed get the grease. Or in this case, the tequila.

They say that idle hands are the devil's playground. It’s true, especially when the idle hands in question are attached to an unsupervised overgrown man-child with a bunch of free time and disposable income burning a hole in his pocket. Once when I was in Europe with Suicidal Tendencies I discovered a big ball of used gaffer's tape over on the side of the stage. Someone must have been pulling up a bunch of old tape from the floor and wrapped the sticky stuff into a good-sized sphere about the size of a grapefruit. We were waiting for showtime as the audience was filing into the venue. I started messing around with the tape ball, tossing it into the air and catching it, just goofing around and passing time until the show was to begin. I looked across the stage (I was hanging out on stage right with our guitar tech Billy) and saw our other guitar tech Dave Lee tuning up his guitars and prepping for the show. I looked at the tape ball and a brilliant thought popped into my head. I would throw the ball across the stage and scare Dave! It would be hilarious! He wouldn't know who did it! It would be so funny!

I reared back and threw the tape ball across the stage towards Dave. It arced high over the drum set and amps and struck him directly in the face. I could not have thrown that tape ball more accurately if my life had depended on it. It was a million-to-one shot. Dave flinched, staggered back and clutched his face with both hands. My eyes bulged as he stumbled in a circle. Good god, did I put his eye out? Finally he pulled his hands away from his face and stared around wildly, looking for the culprit. I was happy to note that both his eyes appeared intact, if a bit watery. I also gratefully noted there was no blood. His watering eyes scanned the audience. Finally his gaze fell on me, looking at him white-faced from across the stage.

He started towards me.

I started looking for an escape route. Seeing none, I started rehearsing my apology. Dave was a big guy, a very nice guy, but even a really nice guy can forget he's so nice when he's just been hit in the eye with a big ball of used duct tape the size of a grapefruit. He came bursting out from behind the amplifiers with the tape ball in his hand and stood looking down at me, breathing heavily. He held up the incriminating tape ball before my eyes.

"Watch out," he said. "They're throwing tape!"

With that he tossed the offending tape ball into a wastebasket and stomped back to his side of the stage.

I don't think I ever confessed this crime to him. Dave, if you're reading this, it was me. And I'm sorry.

On one Alice Cooper tour one of our crew was buddies with Ted Nugent. Ted seemed fond of the guy, which was a good thing, seeing as Ted is A) kinda sorta crazy and B) heavily armed and gleefully adept at the fine art of killing. Terrible Ted shipped us a bunch of his signature archery gear out on the road, including several compound bows, a couple of life-sized animal-shaped targets and enough arrows to get into a whole lot of trouble with. Alice was playing what is commonly referred to as the "sheds" that summer, big open-air pavilions with covered stages and lawn seating areas. These venues also have big parking lots where enterprising roadies can set up archery ranges if they so desire. Seeing as Uncle Ted had sent us this treasure trove of dangerous toys, naturally we set to work creating a deadly playground. We never got ourselves into too much trouble with these potentially lethal toys, but we did get some weird looks from the other bands on the bill when they'd pass by our crew bus and see a life-sized elk riddled with razor tipped hunting arrows hanging out of our luggage bay.

Similarly, Dave Lee (my hapless tape ball target) devised a potato gun made out of PVC tubing and an igniter that used flammable hairspray to launch potatoes out of the stadiums we were working in one summer. If his airborne spuds ever injured someone upon their reentry to earth's atmosphere, we never found out about it. But the folks in catering got pretty tired of him asking for potatoes all day.

Marathon tour bus treks, frequently referred to as "submarine rides", can really make roadies get stir-crazy. It's not uncommon for long rides to take 16 to 18 hours. You can only watch so many movies and take so many drugs before things get weird. Or weirder than usual, anyway. On a European tour with Alice Cooper the band bus and the crew bus were traveling together on one such long trip when both buses pulled into a rest stop. When the band disembarked, some of the roadies sneaked onto their bus and started stealing whatever they could get their hands on. Upon their return the band found ransom notes in place of their missing personal belongings. Poorly spelled and rife with grammatical errors, the messages instructed the hapless rockers that if they ever wanted to see their beloved items alive again to deliver all their alcohol to the crew bus, lest their missing belongings come to a grim end. We thought this prank was hysterical. The band didn't. We ended up getting the booze anyway.

ALL ACCESS
When the driver stops at a truck stop in the middle of a long overnight drive, always let him know if you're getting off the bus to go buy a Snickers bar or whatever. Getting left behind on tour is no joke. Have you ever seen the people hanging out at truck stops at 3am? I'd rather be on a speeding bus full of crazed roadies.

Sometimes tour pranks don't work out so well. On a day off on a Suicidal Tendencies tour Rocky the ST guitarist broke out his rollerblades at the hotel. Rocky is a tremendous hockey fan, as well as a decent hockey player in his own right. The LA Kings, led by Wayne Gretzky, had just been to the Stanley Cup Finals that past summer and California had become Hockeytown overnight. Perhaps inspired by his hometown team's success, Rocky was amusing himself by playing indoor hockey. On the surface, the game is quite simple. You skate up and down the hotel hallways with your hockey stick, knocking on your band-mates doors and start shooting pucks into the room when they open the door. Needless to say, the only one who thought this was funny was Rocky. Soon his fellow rockers had had enough. The hockey game ended prematurely when Rocky fell and grabbed onto the door jamb just as a pissed off hotel-room inhabitant slammed the door closed. Rocky's hand got smashed by the door causing significant damage to the fingers on his right hand. This sort of injury is painful and certainly no fun, but it isn't career ending...unless you're the lead guitarist of a heavy metal band that is in the middle of a world tour. To Rocky's credit, Suicidal only had to cancel one show before he returned to the stage with a surgically repaired picking hand, shredding away on his axe like nothing had even happened. Must have had some kickass pain meds.

23 BACK TO MEGADETH

I got the call to come back and work for Megadeth again in 2001, after finishing out 2000 touring with Alice Cooper and Nina Gordon, and then touring Japan and Australia with KISS in early 2001. Megadeth had just released their first album with Al Pitrelli on guitar, a return to their old school thrash metal roots entitled "The World Needs A Hero." They had an extensive tour booked as they attempted to make a comeback after the disappointing results of the "Risk" album experiment.

Once again Megadeth kicked things off with a string of acoustic shows. These were pretty low key affairs at smaller bars or clubs for an audience of fan club contest winners and radio station bigwigs. We were flying to every show so we logged plenty of hours at airport bars across America. Rather than trying to bring a drum set along on commercial flights Jimmy was having a small drum set provided at every show by local music stores, so I had plenty of logistics to keep track of to ensure we had the right stuff every day. The local providers dropped the ball a few times but luckily Jimmy wasn't too fussy, and as long as he had what he needed to make the gig happen he was usually satisfied. We played a sports grill called "The Hockeyland Cafe" in Detroit, which still stands as the best name for a Megadeth concert venue of all time. Well, that one or "The Liquor Store" in Quebec City. Actually, "The Liquor Store" is way a cooler name.

After about a month and a half of these warm-up gigs we were headed to England to start the European leg of the tour. Megadeth would be opening for rock 'n' roll legends AC/DC in stadiums across Europe, as well as playing the usual summer festival circuit and playing headlining shows in clubs and theatres. In order to make the logistics work out we had to bring two full sets of backline equipment out with us...two drum sets, two sets of guitar amps, two sets of rack gear, two sets of electronic drum triggers, everything.

Logistically, it was a headache. We had the "A" rig for the AC/DC shows and the "B" rig for the festival shows and headlining gigs. It was pretty complicated keeping everything straight. There were some things the band absolutely had to have at every show, like their favorite guitars, pedals, cymbals etc, so we had to carry these essential items with us every time we flew from one setup to the other. We called that stuff the "Universal" gear.

Dealing with the two sets of backline gear was a complete headache. A typical week might go something like this:

> Friday June 8 - Megadeth opens for AC/DC at the Milton Keynes' Bowl (Capacity 55,000) using the "A" rig. After the show we pull the "Universal" gear and fly to Milan Italy to meet up with the waiting "B" rig, bringing the "Universal" gear on the plane with us. Meanwhile the "A" rig is trucked to Hochheim, Germany.

Saturday June 9 - Megadeth performs at the "Gods Of Metal" Festival in Milan, Italy (Capacity 15,000) using the "B" rig. After the show we pull the "Universal" gear and fly to Frankfurt, Germany bringing the "Universal" gear on the plane with us, and then drive 50 miles to Hochheim, Germany to meet up with the waiting "A" rig. Meanwhile the "B" rig is trucked to Macumba, Spain.

Sunday June 10 - Megadeth opens for AC/DC in Hochheim, Germany (Capacity 60,000) using the "A" rig. After the show we pull the "Universal" gear and drive 50 miles back to Frankfurt. Meanwhile the "A" rig is trucked to Cottbuss, Germany.

Monday June 11 - We fly to Madrid, Spain bringing the "Universal" gear on the plane with us and drive to Macumba, Spain to meet the waiting "B" rig. Megadeth performs a headlining show at Club Macumba (Capacity 2,000). After the show we drive 220 miles to Valencia, Spain. No need to pull the "Universal" gear for a change.

Tuesday June 12 - Megadeth performs a headlining show in Madrid at Sala Republica (Capacity 1,700). After the show we drive 220 miles to Barcelona, Spain. Another night off from pulling the "Universal" gear.

> Wednesday June 13 - Megadeth performs a headlining show in Barcelona at Club Razzmatazz (Capacity 2,000). After the show we drive 350 miles to San Sebastian, Spain. We're starting to forget how to pull the "Universal" gear.
>
> Thursday June 14 - Megadeth performs a headlining show in San Sebastian at Polideportivo de Anoeta (Capacity 3,500). After the show we pull the "Universal" gear and drive 60 miles to the Bilbao Airport. Don't know where Bilbao is? There's a good reason for that. We sleep a few hours on the bus, then catch a 6:45 am flight from Bilbao to Madrid bringing the "Universal" gear on the plane with us, then a 9:30am flight from Madrid to Berlin, Germany, again bringing the "Universal" gear on the plane with us.
>
> Friday June 15- Drive 80 miles to Cottbus, Germany to meet up with the waiting "A" rig. Megadeth opens for AC/DC in Cottbus (Capacity 50,000) using the "A" rig. Meanwhile the "B" rig is trucked to Bochum, Germany.

If you thought reading that bullshit schedule sucked, try living it.

The whole European tour was exhausting, both mentally keeping track of what gear was going where, and physically with all the crazy flights and drives from one tour to another.

We hung in there and got the job done every day, somehow. It was probably the Jack Daniels.

The AC/DC shows were incredible. Anyone would be freaked out to be opening up for one of the most influential rock bands of all time. I was especially excited since they are one of my all - time favorite rock 'n' roll bands, and their drummer Phil Rudd was a huge inspiration for me when I first started playing drums way back when. His drumming style was rock solid, in the pocket, with a minimum of flash and very few drum fills. There's a great old saying among rock 'n' roll drummers, "The only 'fill' you need is 'Phil' Rudd." It was incredible to have the chance to see the man himself play every night in front of thousands of fans in those huge stadiums. Another one of my lifelong dreams comes true, thanks to rock 'n' roll!

The AC/DC stage set was a true rock 'n' roll spectacle, with a larger-than-life robotic statue of their lead guitar player that burst through a faux brick wall at the back of the stage during the show. Smoke spewed out of the mouth and flames shot from the end of the guitar. They also had clear plastic sections of the stage so the video crew underneath the stage could shoot up through the floor to give a really unique point of view for the giant video screens. They got some great shots of the band rocking out that the crowd just loved.

AC/DC would open the show with the stage completely dark, then this huge bell was slowly lowered down to the stage with a single red spotlight on it. The crowd goes bananas when they see the bell coming in, because they know what's coming. Brian the singer comes out and starts striking the bell with this big hammer, the intro to their classic track "Hell's Bells." The guitar begins playing the iconic opening riff, and when the rest of the band kicks in with a tremendous pyro blast the entire stadium erupts into rock pandemonium! The band was tight as hell and played all their classic rock anthems. They know what the fans come to see and they definitely deliver it. With so many albums and so many hits every song is a highlight of the show.

At this point the band is getting on in years, so they don't get too crazy on stage - except for the lead guitarist Angus Young. He built his career on his over the top stage performances, and even at his advanced age he is still out there going crazy and whipping the crowds into a frenzy night after night. I don't know how he does it. Wearing his iconic school-boy outfit complete with short pants and cap he struts his stuff for two and a half hours of rock 'n' roll madness, headbanging, duck-walking and throwing himself around the stage with reckless abandon. He even flings himself down on the floor like a petulant child throwing a temper tantrum - and the cameras under the transparent stage floor get it all up onto the video screens for the fans to enjoy. Talk about being all in, Angus is still living his rock 'n' roll dream. What an inspiration!

I finally got to meet my drumming hero Phil Rudd after our last show opening for AC/DC tour in Gothenburg, Sweden. There was a small end of tour party back at the hotel and I got to talk to him for a little while over a pint. He was super chill and really nice. He ended up having some legal problems years later after allegedly making threats to kill someone and drug possession. I was pretty freaked out to hear about this, as Phil had seemed like the nicest guy in the world when I met him. Sometimes people aren't what they seem to be, which is why I am somewhat wary of meeting some of my rock 'n' roll heroes in person.

Once we wrapped up the AC/DC tour we sent the "A" rig back to the US (good riddance!) and continued on with only one set of backline equipment, like a normal rock band. Now it was headlining shows and festivals which are always a lot of fun, even if the working conditions can be a little dodgy at the big festival gigs. That's just the nature of the beast, and the opportunity to break up the monotony of touring by seeing new bands and new faces is worth the hassles of the festival circuit. I got to see a bunch of bands I love at the festivals on this tour, including Cradle Of Filth, Motorhead, Savatage, Judas Priest. I also got to hang with my old buddy Tater, who had done monitors for Alice Cooper and was currently out on the road with Judas Priest. You might remember him as the unfortunate soul who had to try and make sense out of the mismatched and malfunctioning monitor consoles and actually fell off the back of the stage during the middle of a disastrous Alice Cooper Eastern Bloc gig. He's a great guy, one of my best friends from my years on the road, and it was awesome to get to see him again even if it was only for one day. Tater has gone on to become one of the top sound guys in the music business, and all I can say is that he completely deserves it. One of the best parts about working the summer festival circuit in Europe is that we get to see old roadie buddies and catch up every year, even if we aren't on a crew together.

One of my favorite venues to visit on these European tours is the Barrowlands in Glasgow, Scotland. It's a big dance hall style room located in a funky neighborhood with some great fish and chips shops nearby. The load in at Barrowlands is unique because the stage is on the top floor of the six story building. However, there is no elevator, only stairs. The local crew is world renowned for their ability to load in just about any band just as quickly as any other venue with a more conventional load in arrangement. The road cases get to the stage in one of two ways; the local hands carry the gear up the six flights of stairs by hand, or they winch it to the top with a chain hoist. There is a narrow vertical channel between the flights of stairs that the road cases can just barely fit into as they are lifted to the top. I have to admit it is a bit harrowing to see your equipment dangling by a load strap six stories up! If there was ever a mishap the gear would be demolished when it hit the concrete floor. Not to mention that somebody would probably be killed in the process. But in all the times I've been to the Barrowlands their crew has never slipped up. Every road case makes it up to the stage and back down again at the end of the night.

The locals are a tough. Hell, everyone in Scotland is tough, even the little old lady selling fish and chips on the corner. The Scots are an interesting bunch, just hard as nails but really kind and funny in their own rough way. I am told they speak English there, but you could have fooled me. I can never understand a word they're saying.

After the load in is completed the Barrowlands stage crew passes the time with a vigorous game of rough and tumble indoor football, or "soccer" as it's called in the US. These guys play every bit as hard as they work, and even a casual game of "footie" among this close-knit group of friends quickly escalates. Fouls start coming fast and furious, but with no referees things get out of hand quickly. A player gets taken out by a rough tackle and is left to lie on the floor holding his injured knee as his friends continue the game around his prone body. Now that's what is known as teamwork. The injured Scotsman managed to crawl off to relative safety on the side of the room, but not before being nearly trampled to death during a particularly spirited scoring attempt.

Megadeth takes the term "World Tour" seriously, playing in some exotic and far-flung rock 'n' roll locations. After almost ten years on the road I still had a few missing stamps in my passport, which were checked off on this run. For example, did you know that Istanbul, Turkey is a hotbed for thrash rock? Yup. Nothing goes together like thrash metal and Turkish teenagers. 5,000 enthusiastic Turkish metalheads turned out to get their metal on with Megadeth.

The best part of visiting Turkey was the coffee. The Turks make it in their own special way, unfiltered and simmered rather than boiled. It is so strong and bitter that it is usually served with sugar or a sweet on the side to take the edge off. This stuff is not for the faint-hearted! One cup will fuel you through the entire day. The grounds are allowed to settle at the bottom of the cup, so at the end you've got some pure caffeine left, if you're brave enough to drink it all. This stuff will put hair on your chest, which explains most of the Turkish stagehands I saw running around shirtless.

20,000 Greek headbangers turned out at the Rockwave Festival in Athens. This gig was at the Olympic Stadium Velodrome, significant seeing as we were in Greece and all. And visiting Ireland was a thrill. As a huge Thin Lizzy fan it was cool to get to visit Phil Lynott's hometown, Dublin. He was the lead singer and bassist for the influential and totally badass rock band Thin Lizzy, and he died at age 36 after a hard life plagued by drug and alcohol abuse. It was easy to see where his romantic but streetwise lyrics came from after spending some time in that town. Those people had been through so much, but always kept their sense of humor and attitude. And, yes, Irish pubs are as good as they are cracked up to be. We had a blast hanging out after the show in Dublin. It was so great to get the opportunity to visit these new places and have such amazing experiences.

One of the best parts about working for heavy metal bands is how appreciative the fans are. With some other genres of music the fans have more of a "take it or leave it" attitude. But the metalheads are appreciative to the extreme, especially in the more remote areas of the planet that don't get big touring bands passing through very often. For these people seeing Megadeth playing in their home town is like a lifelong dream come true, and they aren't shy about expressing their loyalty and dedication. The crowds were insane at these types of shows, with all the stage diving, slam dancing, head banging and moshing that you see in the US or Europe. More insane, really, as the crowds in these underserved areas are trying extra hard to emulate the audiences in the rest of the world. They really take it to the next level. These metalheads are all in and support their favorite bands 100%.

Speaking of remote locations, this was also my first visit to the Pacific Rim. Japan, Australia and New Zealand had all been rocked previously, but Megadeth took this tour to South Korea, Taiwan, Indonesia and Malaysia, places I had never visited before. Hell, just finding them on a map was a challenge! But thanks to the gods of rock 'n' roll, our hero gets to go there and make more roadie dreams come true. When they named the album "The World Needs A Hero" they apparently meant the *entire* world! It was a really unique experience to play these places. It was a lot like playing in the Eastern Bloc countries: the concert support staff were super enthusiastic and sincerely doing their best, but it never really cut it. Outdated sound equipment, inadequate power, small stages, rainy weather, inexperienced production staff...suffice it to say there were many, many challenges making the shows happen the way the band expects them to during the Pacific Rim dates. Megadeth are true pros and always delivered the goods on stage no matter how screwed up things got, and I'm always grateful for Jimmy Degrasso's good attitude. Luckily our guitar techs always had a bottle of Jack Daniels in their road cases for an after show drink, which was desperately needed after some of these more problematic shows!

The Pacific Rim is infamous for its deadly tropical storms. One such killer storm was moving through Malaysia while we were there, which made for some harrowing air travel. Our Kuala Lumpur concert was canceled because of the bad weather. We had a choice: try to get to Medan in Indonesia before the storm hit to do our final Pacific Rim concert, or play it safe and bypass the whole mess to start the Australian leg of the tour. Tour manager Steve decided to cancel the Medan show and head for Sydney. Turns out it was the right decision as the tropical storm escalated to a Category 1 hurricane and made landfall in Medan right around the time we would have been arriving.

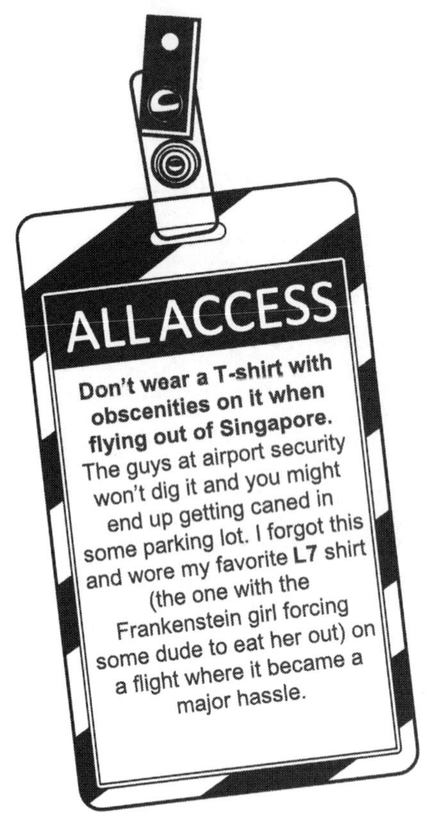

ALL ACCESS
Don't wear a T-shirt with obscenities on it when flying out of Singapore.
The guys at airport security won't dig it and you might end up getting caned in some parking lot. I forgot this and wore my favorite L7 shirt (the one with the Frankenstein girl forcing some dude to eat her out) on a flight where it became a major hassle.

Megadeth, like most heavy metal bands, are way more popular overseas than they are in the USA. After a reasonably successful tour abroad the band returned to their home country for a coast-to coast US tour. After the "Risk" fiasco this time around their booking agent booked the band into smaller venues. In the music business these are frequently referred to as "intimate settings." If some of these places got any more intimate there wouldn't be room for the drum set on stage. However, the close quarters seemed to fit in with the band's efforts to reconnect with their thrash metal roots, and having the crowds right on top of us in these smaller clubs definitely ratcheted up the intensity factor at the gigs. When the mosh pit is basically on stage things tend to get fierce.

After so many years on the road I had worked at most of the places we were booked at on this tour before. For instance, we played the Roseland in Portland, the same place I got fired on my last time through with Megadeth.

Then everything changed for everyone living in America. After the Portland show on September 9 we headed to Seattle for a day off and then a show at the Showbox Theatre on September 11, 2001. Waking up in a hotel room nursing a low grade hangover from an evening out in one of my favorite cities, I turned on the TV in my hotel room and saw the news that would change the world. The World Trade Center towers in New York City had been destroyed by airplanes crashing into them. At this point nobody had imagined that the type of terrorist attacks that happened with sickening regularity around the rest of the world could ever happen here in America. We were wrong. As the horrifying details unfolded we all got a phone call from Steve the tour manager. The Seattle show had been cancelled and we were headed directly to Vancouver for our next show on the schedule. I walked around outside the hotel for a while before the bus was scheduled to depart for Canada to try to get my shit together.

Downtown Seattle was like a ghost town. Nobody was on the streets, it made a suitably eerie backdrop for one of the worst days in US history. It was a subdued and frightened group of roadies that boarded the tour bus that afternoon to head for Vancouver. Amazingly we had no trouble getting into Canada. This was before the US developed lockdown tactics and terrorism procedures. The whole country was still trying to get their heads wrapped around what had just happened. On the bus ride to Vancouver Sal, our guitar tech, was inconsolable. Like Al Pitrelli, he was a native New Yorker and he was in shock, wondering about his friends and family a continent away. Smart phones hadn't been invented yet and news was slow coming in, and communication with the East Coast from a moving tour bus was still impossible.

Somehow the country moved forward, and so did our little rock 'n' roll tour. Sal and Al were able to contact their people back East and make sure they were safe. The President made an appeal to the American people not to be afraid to continue their ordinary daily routines. He urged people to go on with their lives and not let the terrorists intimidate them. Crowds at the Megadeth shows actually seemed to pick up a little after 9-11 so maybe it worked. Dave got his guitar painted with an American flag and started including some pretty patriotic speech in his onstage banter with the audiences that went over well in this harsh new world. We couldn't have possibly known then where things would go.

The crazy reality of the 9-11 attacks really put the rest of our lives in new perspective. Did my concerns about how many concert tickets Megadeth sold for their show at a sports bar in some one horse town really matter when 3,000 people had just been murdered? It made me start thinking hard about what was really important to me. The idea of being out on the road devoting all my energy to making a rock concert happen started to seem kind of pointless. For the first time in my touring career I wasn't sure if I was in the right place. And the fact that we were playing some really crummy places with indifferent ticket sales didn't help matters much. Our show on Halloween night was especially depressing. We were playing at the Bases Loaded Sports Bar in Wausau, Wisconsin, and no, that name is not made up. I believe this place also had an indoor sand volleyball court if memory serves. By this point I was self-medicating pretty heavily with alcohol to get through the days. The venue was located in a picturesque strip mall, and was about as far away from heavy metal heaven as you could get. The place was half full, everyone on the tour was miserable and wondering what was going to happen next. I was talking to my new girlfriend Kristina back in Arizona on the phone and thinking to myself, what am I doing here? I would rather be home. The whole thing started feeling like going through the motions. The exact opposite of being all in.

The tour was scheduled to finish up in Arizona with two nights of audio and video recording for a live album/DVD project in Tucson and Phoenix. A live recording or video shoot is like a combination of a live concert and a studio recording session all in one. The performance should to be a faithful representation of the band at that moment in time, but you also want it to sound and look as perfect as possible, as this will be out there forever. Lots of bands go into the studio later to clean up the live recording by overdubbing additional tracks to fill out the sound or fix the inevitable mistakes that happen when a band is running around on stage amped up on adrenaline and god knows what else during a rock 'n' roll show. They call this "sweetening" and believe me, some of your favorite live albums are plenty sweet.

Part of a drum tech's gig is to serve as a sort of stand-in for the drummer and do all the boring crap no rock star in his right mind would want to do, like polish cymbals, change drum heads or hit the snare drum two bazillion times while the sound engineers get things sounding right. It was all part of a marathon soundcheck to get the audio right for both the live PA system and the recording truck. Throw in tuning and retuning what seemed like every piece of the kit several times at the behest of the sound crew and my arms were ready to fall off by the time we got the whole drum set on point.

The first show in Tucson was pretty special for me, it was the first time I had done a Megadeth gig in my adopted hometown. It was kind of a tune-up gig for the band as they prepped for the grand finale of the tour in their hometown of Phoenix. But for me it was great to see those familiar faces again after a long and weird road trip. The band pulled out all the stops, and if you've seen the DVD you have to admit it really is the best that band has ever been. They had been through the fire and come out the other side.

24 THIS IS THE END

Most guys can never break away from the touring life. After a while it becomes such a deep part of you that it's impossible to leave behind. All your friends are on the road. You become used to those big paychecks, and your standard of living goes up to the point where you could never maintain it doing anything else. Well, anything else that you're qualified for, anyway. Some guys can transition from being a roadie to a straight job in the real world. Usually it's doing local concert production or studio recording services, musical instrument repair or other entertainment related gigs. I made that same move after meeting the woman who eventually became my wife.

After the Megadeth video shoot and live album project ended I was out of work for several months. The music business can be that way; one minute you're working non-stop, the next you're sitting home wondering if you'll ever be back on tour again. While I was home in Arizona I scored a gig at a local casino doing event and concert production to fill the gap until my phone rang with another tour. The job was fun, I got to maintain my rock 'n' roll work ethic, and it paid decent money - although nowhere near what I was making as a roadie. Still, it was nice to have a steady paycheck and get a chance to stay in one spot for a change. My personal life was changing too. Things were getting serious with my girlfriend Kristina. We had met when a band

I was playing in practiced in the same rehearsal space that her band was using. Yes, of course she's a rocker! Did you expect anything else? Kristina was the guitarist and singer in a Tucson band called Cloven Hoof. We hit it off right away and things took off from there. As my hiatus from the road stretched on we fell in love and decided to make a life together. I wasn't sure how this would impact my life as a roadie and I didn't really care at the moment. Things were going so great I didn't want to change anything. I moved in with Kristina and her child, and before we knew it another kid was on the way, our son Troy.

ALL ACCESS
Think of others. Don't hog up all the stagehands. The other guys on the crew need help too. I used to monopolize the local hands to do all my grunt work (polishing cymbals, cleaning drums, rotating the wheels on my skateboard) until the other guys let me know it **WAS NOT COOL**. The roadie crew is a **team**, act like it.

By this time I had turned down several offers to go back on tour, from some pretty big name groups - Linkin Park, Godsmack and Alice Cooper had all inquired about my services. But I turned them all down, as I had a such a good thing going at home.

After all those years of living my rock 'n' roll roadie dream I was surprised to discover that my dream had changed. Waking up to the same faces every day and having a "normal life" wasn't as bad as I thought it would be. Especially once

Troy arrived. I had that familiar feeling of being in the right place at the right time, only now instead of feeling that way about touring the world with a rock 'n' roll band, being a dad inspired that wonderful feeling in me.

But just when I thought I was out of the music business for good, they pulled me back in. In 2006 Eric Singer contacted me and asked if I was available to drum tech for him for a short Japanese tour with KISS. At this point I had been off the road for over three years. I was rusty as hell. In order to go I'd have to burn all my vacation time at the casino for the entire year. It would put my wife in a really tight spot taking care of our family solo while I was off in Japan.

Despite all that, I managed to get the time off from work and agreed to do the gig. There were many reasons: Eric Singer is probably the nicest guy anyone could work for in this business, KISS takes great care of their crew, the payday would be very, very good, and I love Japan. But most of all, deep down I missed being on the road. It was still a part of me, and I wanted that feeling again.

I connected with Eric to sort out the details for his drums and other gear. These gigs weren't part of an extensive world tour, just a short string of dates, so instead of shipping his drums over to Japan, Pearl drums would be providing his gear locally for the tour. I contacted Eric's equipment sponsors and coordinated everything we would need; drums, cases, sticks, heads, hardware, cymbals and all.

One long plane ride later and it was back to my old stomping grounds: Rainbow Hall in Nagoya, Japan. Upon arrival it was great to see all the familiar faces on the road crew from the last KISS tour. However, it was kind of weird to just walk in cold and start getting ready for the first show. And to be using gear that we had never seen before made me a little anxious as well. On normal tours there is plenty of spare stuff in case something goes wrong. And most of the time we'll do rehearsals and have some time to sort out the equipment. Here it was a matter of hit the ground running. No safety net.

I found the pile of cases that had been shipped to the venue for Eric and started opening them up to check out the gear. The drums all looked good and I changed out the heads and got them cleaned up. I couldn't locate any cymbals, however. I searched the venue, checking all the likely places they might be, like the loading dock, the production office and so on. No luck. As it got closer to sound-check time I started to freak out. Tracking them down was made more difficult by the language barrier. I was able to get a phone call made to the local equipment supplier and discovered that the cymbals had been sent to the wrong city by accident. There was a guy on the bullet train coming to Nagoya with them now, he'd be there in about an hour. And of course, sound-check was supposed to start in about an hour.

I gave Patrick the production manager the bad news. He wasn't happy but didn't freak out. He's basically a rock roadie Hall Of Fame legend and this wasn't his first rodeo. I did what I could - I got all the rest of Eric's drums set up except for the cymbals, then positioned myself by the back door to see what would arrive first, the band or the cymbals. If it was the cymbals I'd need to haul ass to the stage, set them up and hope they were the stuff we had asked for. There wasn't much of a margin for error. If the band arrived first I'd be explaining to Gene Simmons why his drummer didn't have any cymbals. If that happened I'd most likely be unemployed and flying back to Arizona that evening.

As fate would have it, the cymbals arrived first. I grabbed the case from the rep from the backline company and ran for the stage. Opening the case, I was relieved to see they had sent all the correct sizes and models we had requested. At least it was the right stuff! I was putting the last couple of cymbals on the stands when Eric came up to the drum riser. I had barely made it.

Sound-check went as smoothly as can be expected. Without the benefit of any sort of production rehearsals everyone on the crew was in the same boat as I was. Except for the part about not having your stuff. But the KISS crew is always made up of the top people in the industry and everyone handled their business like true professionals.

As you know from my last time with these guys, there are many moving parts to coordinate for a KISS show, which is really different from working for most bands. Besides the usual sound, lighting, backline and staging, KISS also had their usual pyrotechnics, video, costumes, makeup, the famous lighted KISS sign, and extensive special effects. And lots of 'em. All the classic KISS gags I remembered from last time were back again for this tour. The drum riser rises up out of the stage. The band is lowered down from the lighting truss overhead. Gene flies up to the lighting truss on a wire. Paul flies out to a mini-stage in the middle of the audience. Eric plays his drum solo with flaming drumsticks. Tommy launches rockets from his exploding guitar and destroys the lighting rig overhead. Confetti cannons. Fire breathing. Tee shirt cannons. Blood spitting. You name it. I swear there's a kitchen sink out there at some point.

As I already knew, Eric also sings. A lot. Singing drummers can be a pain to work with under the best circumstances. Eric takes it one step further with that special boom microphone stand of his that must be swung in when he wants to sing and back out when he's finished, so he can rock out. It takes some pretty precise timing and an intimate knowledge of the KISS songs. Luckily most of the songs on the set list were KISS live concert staples that I was familiar with already from my last go-round with this bunch. As always, the main trick was not giving him a bloody nose when the microphone came flying in.

After the Nagoya show I packed up as fast as I could. It was a bit wonky as all the loaner drums came with individual cases. Normally Eric has big trap cases that have individual compartments for each drum so I just chuck 'em all in and close the latch. Done! With this loaner gear I had to open up a small case, put in the drum, and buckle the strap back up. Multiply that by about a dozen drums. It added a considerable amount of time to my tear-down. Plus I was out of roadie-shape. I hadn't done a real rock 'n' roll tour in several years, and it showed. I was the last guy ready to pack the truck and I definitely caught some heat from the stage manager for it.

I eventually got my feet under me and got into a better rhythm so at least I wasn't totally fucking up load out anymore. Japan was, as always, a blast, despite the rainy weather that dogged us. The people, the lights, the big cities, the language, the food, it's always been one of my favorite places to visit.

After the first show we found out KISS was adding a one-off show back in the USA at Chumash Casino in California at the end of the Japanese dates. This was a problem for me. I was supposed to be going back at work at MY casino. I think I was probably the only roadie in rock history for whom working for KISS was a side hustle. I told management about my dilemma, and they weren't too happy. Now they had to track down somebody back in the USA to handle the single Chumash gig, and coordinate a bunch of extra details. I became fairly unpopular fairly quickly.

Working with Eric was a pleasure as always. The guy is funny, easy-going and the best rock 'n' roll drummer I've ever had the pleasure of lighting a pair of drumsticks on fire for. It goes without saying that working for KISS was a tremendous honor. Sadly, it was rapidly becoming clear that I was in the wrong place. This wasn't who I was, not anymore. I wasn't all in. I was living in two worlds. I had a family and a career back home. I had new dreams that didn't fit here anymore. I didn't belong out here with people who were 100%

invested in what we were doing. I sucked it up, did my best, and made it through the rest of the Japanese gigs.

When the tour ended, for the first time ever, going home was a relief.

25 EPILOGUE

The day my son was born in 2003 was the happiest day of my life. I had always dreamed of having a family, being a husband and father, and that was finally all happening. I was 37 and had a great life with my wife Kristina. And now I was a dad.

Being a father affected me deeply. I was very excited about being a father, but scared too. I was afraid I was going to screw it up somehow! I didn't have the greatest example to follow; my parents split up when I was very young and both had their own demons to battle. I didn't remember my own childhood very fondly, and I really wanted to do things differently and give my son the life I didn't have as a boy. I was kind of looking for father role models, or somewhere to discover what being a good father looked like.

I eventually fell in with a rough crowd - right wing conservative radio ushered me into their idea of fatherhood, family & America. It made sense on some levels...stability, tradition, and security were all part of the talking points that appealed to me. All stuff a worried new father would want for his child. This was bound to cause some problems in my life for a variety of reasons. My wife and the mother of my child is a lifelong liberal democrat, very progressive socially, religiously, and culturally. Over the years the split between our views widened greatly. Our family life seemed normal and stable on the surface. We made our way through the busy life of a modern family; work, school, chores, life. We argued, but not excessively. Nobody had an affair, to the best of my knowledge. But my wife and I didn't do much together outside of family obligations, I was focused strongly on my son, determined to get this "dad thing" right, and seeking guidance where I found it. We kept separate schedules for the most part. I got up early and went to bed late, self-medicating copiously with alcohol. We saw each other for an hour in the morning, a couple of hours at night, and intermittently on weekends. I mostly did things with our son on weekends while she attended yoga classes and other activities. I abandoned, for the most part, compassion and replaced it with fear and a need for security and order. Looking back at it I see how foolish I was. But at the time it made sense for me somehow.

What else was going on? My step-daughter graduated from high school and was about to start college, and my son turned ten years old. These events affected me more than I realized. I had spent a decade or so building my world around people who were now becoming their own people. My family was growing up and change was on the horizon, a change I was grossly unprepared for.

My darkest hour came in late May, 2013. I was 47. My wife was away on a three day trip over the weekend and I was home with our son. I took him to a baseball game and ended up getting a terrible case of food poisoning. By the time we made it back home after the game I was vomiting and feverish. While I was semi-delirious I saw a possible future that really scared me...looking back the closest thing I can compare it to is a vision quest. I know that sounds crazy, but it's the closest thing I can come up with. Or maybe it was more like Scrooge's experience in "A Christmas Carol". I saw that my step-daughter COULD indeed move away and be out of my life. She was starting college and everything in her life was about to change, in a huge way. My son COULD grow up and move out of my life. He was growing up so fast, it seemed like yesterday he was just a baby, and now he was in fifth grade already. And my wife COULD have a life without me in it. Who could blame her for wanting to, with the way I had been treating her? I looked into my fevered dreams and saw a future where I was alone and without the family I had tried so long and so misguidedly to take care of.

ALL ACCESS
MY ROCK-N-ROLL HEROES I'LL NEVER GET TO HANG OUT WITH:
· Philthy Animal Taylor - Motorhead
· Joey Ramone - The Ramones
· Dee Dee Ramone - The Ramones
· Bon Scott - AC/DC

This future terrified me.

The fever broke, and Kristina returned home. I started thinking of ways to build some bridges between my wife and me. I didn't want to be one of those couples who split up after the last child had left the house. For a while there I had thought that was maybe what I wanted. In some ways I was actually looking forward to a "fresh start" once the kids were grown. But when I looked at that scenario up close and in front of me I knew it wasn't what I wanted at all. My wife is an incredible woman and I wanted her with me always.

I started small...with the iconic Date Night. I asked my wife to go to the movies. I tossed in a remark about "saving our marriage" which she kind of laughed off. We had a good time, it was so wonderful to get some together time. I hadn't realized how much I missed being alone with her, without work, chores, kids, just us two and some coffee. I started reorganizing my priorities to make more time for spending time with Kristina. I started looking for the things that attracted me to her when we first met. I had been dabbling in yoga for a few years (it really helped me after I started suffering from terrible back pain) and out of nowhere Kristina invited me to start going to her yoga class on Saturday mornings. It's a really cool yoga class, it's kind of like that movie "Fight Club" - class is held at the instructor's guest house, and she doesn't advertise, you have to know someone who is a member to get in!

I also took a long hard look at all my belief systems to see what was working for me and what wasn't. Everything was on the table - religion, politics, cultural beliefs, food, sex, you name it. Nothing was held sacred as I went through all of my ideals to determine if they were really serving me. I started tossing some of my long held beliefs and trying to look at things around me more rationally and with an open-mind. To be honest I was kind of embarrassed about some of the stuff I was into, when I looked at it clearly and unflinchingly. In short order I found myself studying Buddhist philosophy and eating a vegetarian diet. Weird, right? It was a big change from my days as a carnivorous rock 'n' roll roadie demolishing a platter of wings and a pitcher of Budweiser every chance he got. My politics took a left turn as well. And my relationship with my wife kept getting better in many ways.

I also found myself losing weight. I ended up losing about 40 pounds in four or five months, from my heaviest weight of 206 down to where I am now at around 160. I never really went on any kind of specific diet or exercise regimen consciously, but I did make an effort to stop clouding my mind with alcohol every night, and I chose to stop eating fast food. I had been a frequent visitor to the drive through windows of Tucson! I also stopped eating meat – mostly. I still don't count pizza toppings as meat. And neither should you, because pepperoni pizza is delicious! I'm actually experimenting with going vegan at this point. And I was meditating and doing yoga every morning, and being more mindful in general.

I got some push back from some of my friends who liked the old fat roadie Jeff better than the new skinny hippie Jeff. But mostly people were supportive and happy for me. I think I might have even inspired a few people along the way to make some changes in their own lives. Looking back it was a pretty radical turnabout. It all just kind of happened, which was the strange thing. It all started with that weird vision quest. Things are still not perfect. They never will be! But are things better? Yes.

I still stay in touch with some of my rock 'n' roll friends from my years on tour, especially Ken Barr, who inspired me to write this book and whose guidance and assistance in this effort have been invaluable. If it wasn't for you, Ken, I would never have been able to get this thing done. I get Christmas cards from Eric Singer. Well, they're actually KISS-mas cards, but you get the idea. Toby Mamis still gets me into Alice Cooper shows when the gang passes through Arizona on tour. Thanks to my friends in the business my kids have seen some great gigs and my son still has those Jimmy Degrasso drum sticks he got backstage at an Alice Cooper show. I'm still head over heels in love with rock music, and I'm so grateful my rock 'n' roll roadie dream came true. I will never forget my life on the road and that feeling of being in just the right place at just the right time. That feeling of being all in.

ACKNOWLEDGMENTS

Thanks to Ken Barr for inspiring me to write this book and for his invaluable guidance throughout this project.

Thanks to Eric Singer, Jimmy Degrasso, Josh Freese, Steve Klong, Ken Jay, Steve Scully, Vinnie Ludovico and Ginger Baker for giving me the opportunity to change your drum heads and play your drums when you weren't around.

Thanks to Tom Abraham for getting me my first big rock tour.

Thanks to Scott Sterling for taking me under your wing and teaching me what rock 'n' roll is really all about.

Thanks to Shane Preston for letting me crash on your sofa all those times.

Thanks to ROGO for the amazing artwork and inspiration.

Thanks to Zoe and Brian for editing and making this thing readable. Your feedback was wonderful and kept me going through to the end.

Thanks to Kristina for giving me a reason to find a new dream. And thanks to Troy and Dev for making that dream even more awesome-er. I love you guys.

Finally, thanks to all my roadie brothers and sisters I toured with over the years, and to those who are still out there on the road. You're the ones who are really ALL IN.

THE BOOK ROADIES

Rich “Rogo” Rogowski: Art Director, Illustrator and Designer

Zohannah Reeves and Brian Winkler: Editorial Overlords

Camine Zapperoli: Creative Consultant

Deni Gardner: Technical Advisor

RESOURCES

Get more information at: therealjeffmann.com

Read my blog at: lazyace.svbtle.com

See more of Rogo’s amazing art at: rogoillo.weebly.com

ABOUT THE AUTHOR

Jeff Mann fled the ice and snow of upstate NY in 1992 to pursue his dreams. After 10 years traveling around the world as a roadie for touring rock bands, he now writes about rock 'n' roll, current events, politics and the world around us...from his own warped perspective, of course. In his spare time he referees roller derby and enjoys reading, tattoos, beer, travel, yoga and spending time with his wife and children. He is a recovering drummer currently living in Tucson, Arizona.

THE

END

JEFF MANN WILL RETURN

IN HIS UPCOMING BOOK:

“THE ZEBRA DIARIES: REFFING ROLLER DERBY BE HARD”

OKAY, THIS IS REALLY
THE END OF THE BOOK NOW

Made in the USA
Middletown, DE
03 January 2018